OPERATING SYSTEM AND UNIX

S. Gayathiri | S. Priyadarshini | N.S. Usha

KHANNA BOOK PUBLISHING CO. (P) Ltd.
4C/4344, Ansari Road, Darya Ganj, New Delhi, India

Sathyabama Institute of Science and Technology
Jeppiaar Nagar, Rajiv Gandhi Salai, Chennai, Tamilnadu, India

Dear Readers,

To prevent the piracy, this book is secured with HIGH SECURITY HOLOGRAM on the front title cover. In case you don't find the hologram on the front cover title, please write us to at contact@khannabooks.com or whatsapp us at +91-99109 09320 and avail special gift voucher for yourself.

Specimen of Hologram on front Cover title:

Enlargement Of Overlay

Moreover, there is a SPECIAL DISCOUNT COUPON for you with EVERY HOLOGRAM.

How to avail this SPECIAL DISCOUNT:

Step 1: Scratch the hologram
Step 2: Under the scratch area, your "coupon code" is available
Step 3: Logon to www.khannabooks.com
Step 4: Use your "coupon code" in the shopping cart and get your copy at a special discount
Step 5: Enjoy your reading!

Thanks,
Khanna Publishing House

ISBN: 978-93-55388-90-2

Operating System and Unix
by **S. Gayathiri; S. Priyadarshini; N.S. Usha**

First Edition: 2025
Reprint: 2026

To view complete list of books, please scan the QR Code:

Published by:
Khanna Book Publishing Co. (P) Ltd.
CIN: U22110DL1998PTC095547

Visit us at: www.khannabooks.com
Write us at: contact@khannabooks.com

Printed in Bharat.

Preface

Operating systems are the backbone of modern computing, managing hardware resources, enabling multitasking, and providing a platform for software applications. Among the various operating systems developed over the decades, Unix has played a pivotal role in shaping the landscape of computing. Its design principles, such as modularity, simplicity, and portability, have influenced many modern operating systems, including Linux and macOS.

This book is designed for undergraduate students who are beginning their journey into the world of operating systems and Unix. It provides a structured introduction to key OS concepts, such as process management, memory management, file systems, and input/output operations, while also offering practical exposure to Unix-based environments. Through a combination of theoretical discussions and hands-on exercises, students will gain both a conceptual understanding and practical skills in working with Unix systems.

The book is structured to cater to students with varying levels of prior exposure to operating systems. Early chapters cover foundational topics, ensuring that readers without prior experience can grasp essential concepts. As the book progresses, it introduces more advanced topics such as system calls, shell scripting, and OS-level programming in Unix. Each chapter is supplemented with examples, exercises, and real-world applications to reinforce learning.

By the end of this book, students will have a solid understanding of how operating systems function and how Unix-based systems operate in practice. This knowledge will not only be valuable for academic success but also serve as a strong foundation for careers in software development, system administration, cybersecurity, and other computing-related fields.

We hope this book makes your learning experience engaging, insightful, and rewarding.

Contents

◆◆◆

UNIT 1

Operating Systems

1.1 OPERATING SYSTEMS

An operating system is essential software that enables a computer to function by managing both its hardware and software resources. It serves as a bridge between the user and the computer's internal components, providing an interface that allows users to interact with the system.

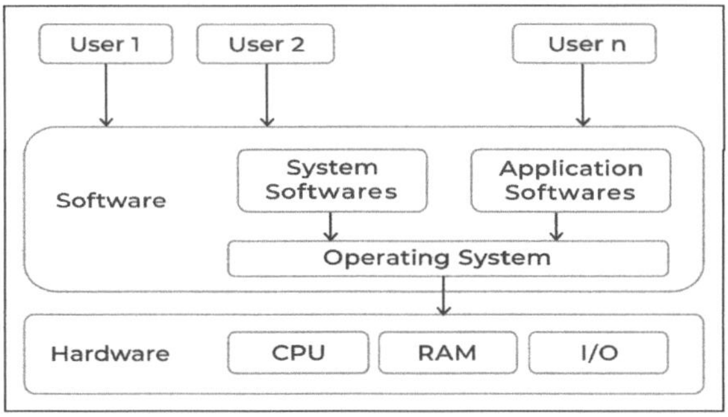

Fig.1.1: *Components in Computer System*

OS Goals

Key goals include:

- **Resource Management:** Allocating CPU, memory, and storage effectively.
- **Process Management:** Overseeing process execution and multitasking.
- **Memory Management:** Allocating and protecting system memory for processes.
- **Security:** Protecting data and preventing unauthorized access.
- **File Management:** Organizing and controlling file storage and access.
- **User Interface:** Providing an easy way for users to interact with the system.
- **Reliability:** Detecting errors and maintaining system stability.
- **Performance Optimization:** Enhancing system speed and efficiency.

The OS controls various aspects such as memory management, process execution, file storage, and input/output operations. In addition to these core functions, operating systems ensure efficient execution of applications by allocating system resources like CPU time and memory. They also provide security features to protect data and prevent unauthorized access. Overall, the operating system's role is to streamline interaction with computer hardware, enabling users and software programs to perform tasks in a seamless and effective manner.

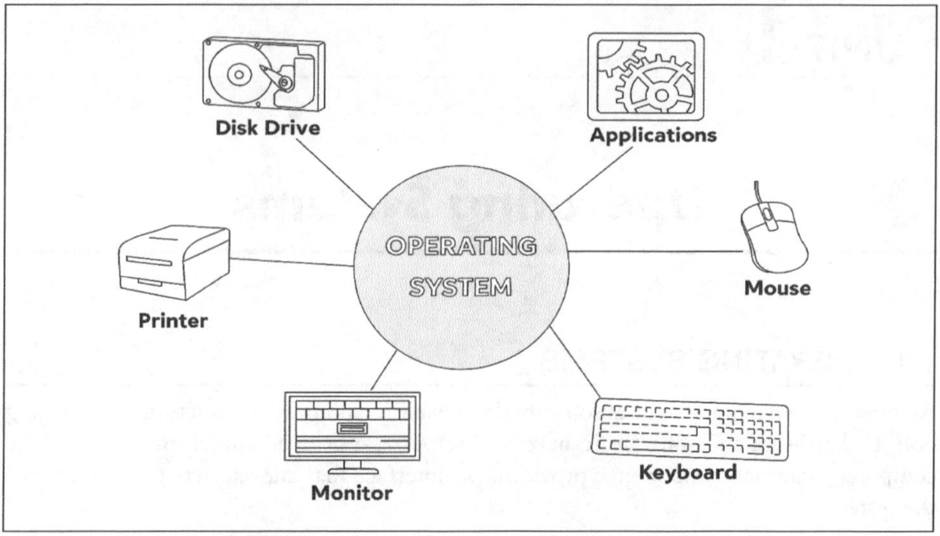

Fig. 1.2: *Interaction of Operating System*

Classification of OS

Multi-user OS

Programs can be run concurrently by many users on a multi-user operating system. The number of users that this kind of system can accommodate at once can range from a few to hundreds or even thousands.

Multiprocessing OS

This operating system enables a program to run on more than one CPU simultaneously.

Multitasking OS

A multitasking operating system allows more than one program to run at once, improving productivity and user experience by managing multiple tasks in parallel.

Multi-threading OS

Operating systems that support multi-threading enable various parts of a single program to run simultaneously. This can improve performance by running multiple program components simultaneously.

Real-time OS

Operating systems that operate in real-time are made to process and react to inputs instantly.

1.2 STRUCTURES

Operating System Structures

Operating systems are structured in various ways to manage and execute programs effectively. The design process involves careful planning to meet specific goals, and OS structure can be viewed through the services provided, user interfaces, and internal components.

1.2.1 Simple Structure

Early OS like MS-DOS were simple and small, designed to be efficient with minimal resources. However, they lacked a well-defined structure, and as they grew, the separation of functions became unclear.

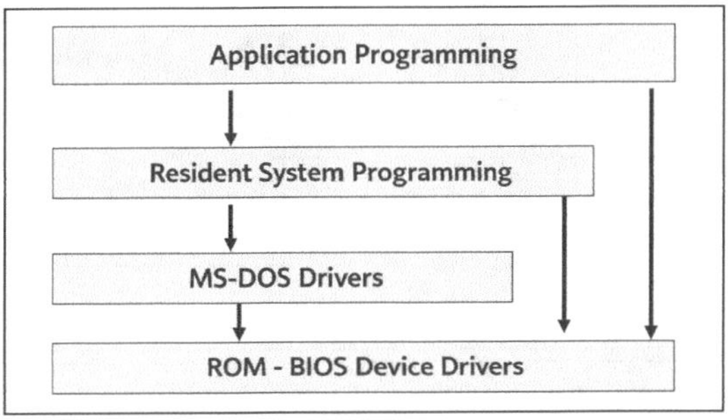

Fig. 1.3: *MS-DOS Structure*

1.2.2 Layered Structure

In this approach, the OS is divided into distinct layers, where each layer depends on the one below it. The lowest layer is hardware, and the top layer is the user interface. While this structure simplifies debugging, it can lead to performance issues as system calls need to pass through multiple layers.

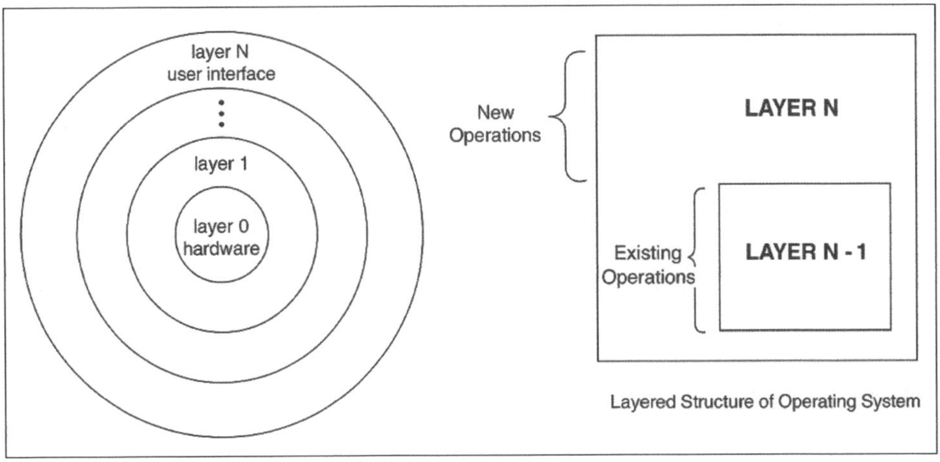

Fig. 1.4: *Layered structure*

Example Layers

- **Layer 5:** User programs
- **Layer 4:** I/O buffering
- **Layer 3:** Device drivers
- **Layer 2:** Memory management
- **Layer 1:** CPU scheduling
- **Layer 0:** Hardware

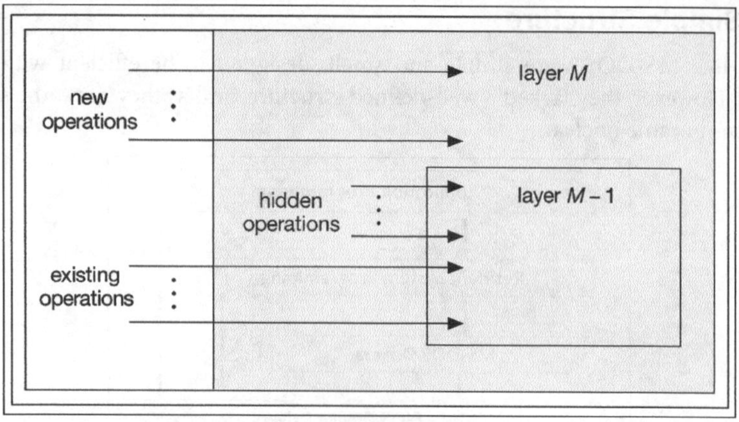

Fig. 1.5: *Operating System Layer*

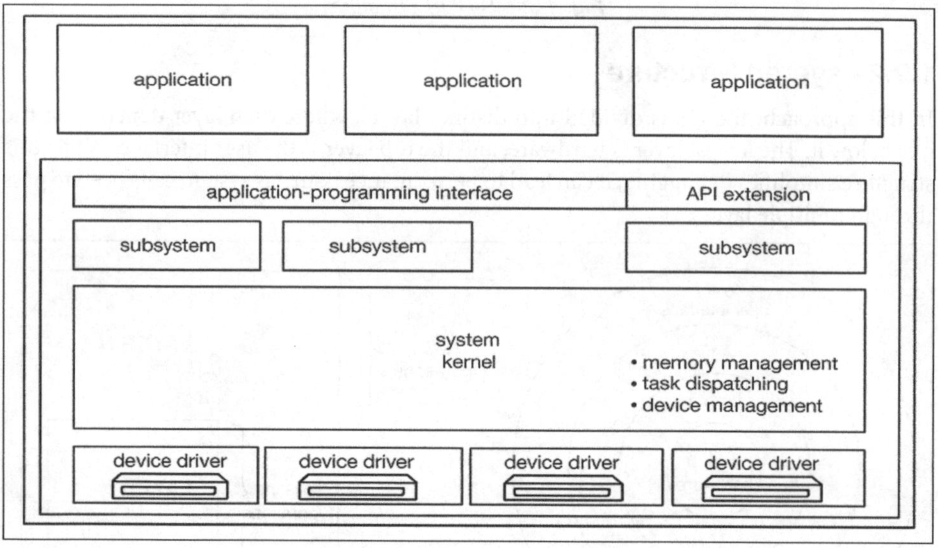

Fig. 1.6: *OS/2 Layer Structure*

1.2.3 Microkernel Structure

Micro-kernels minimize the kernel's functions by moving non-essential services to user space, making the OS modular, secure, and easier to port across different hardware. However, the increased communication overhead can reduce performance.

Advantages of Micro-kernels

- Easier to extend and modify
- Improved security and reliability
- Portability across different architectures

Disadvantages

- Performance can be impacted by message passing between components.

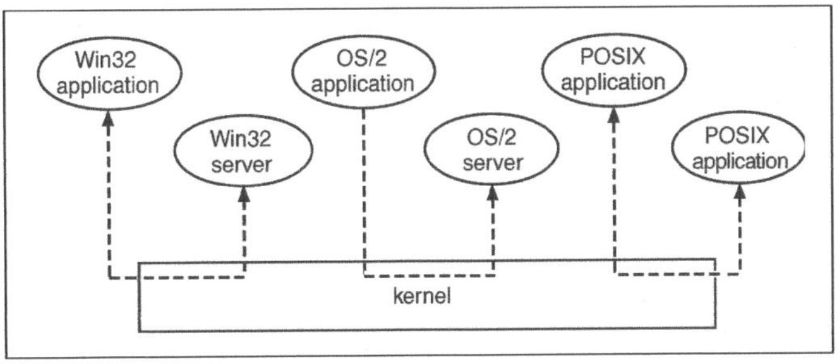

Fig. 1.7: Windows NT Client-Server Structure

1.2.4 Structure of UNIX

The original UNIX operating system was constrained by the hardware capabilities, and its structure was initially quite basic. UNIX can be divided into two main components:

1. System Programs
2. The Kernel
    - The kernel is further subdivided into different device drivers and interfaces, which have been continuously improved and expanded as UNIX has evolved over time.
    - Everything beneath the system call interface and above the physical hardware is considered part of the kernel.
    - The kernel manages crucial functions like file systems, CPU scheduling, memory management, and other operating system tasks via system calls.

Collectively, this represents a vast array of functionality integrated into a single layer. The monolithic design of UNIX made it complex to implement and maintain, as modifications in one area could have unintended consequences on other parts of the system.

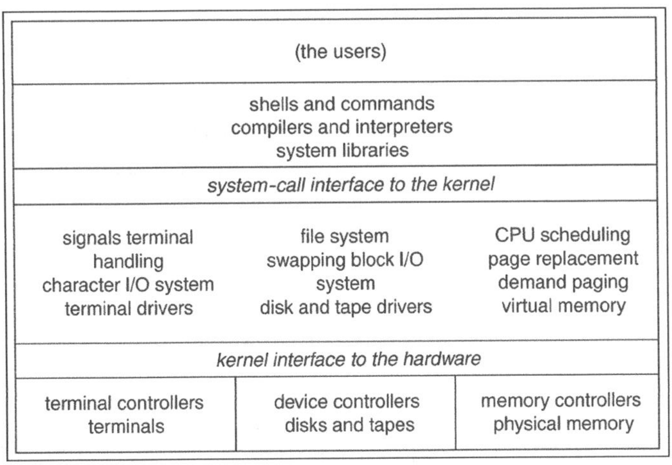

Fig. 1.8: UNIX Structure

The goal of new UNIX versions is to use increasingly sophisticated hardware capabilities. Operating systems can be divided into more manageable, smaller segments with sufficient hardware support, unlike previous MS-DOS or UNIX versions. With this method, the operating system can exert more control over the computer and the programs that run on it. Developers are given greater freedom to design modular operating systems and alter the core structure of the system. The general functions and features are specified and divided into discrete parts using a top-down design. As long as the external interface is constant and the routine completes its intended function, this separation enables programmers to encapsulate details and construct low-level procedures.

Virtual Machine

Every process in a virtual machine environment seems to operate on a separate, dedicated processor with its own memory, hardware, and other resources. All processes share the resources of the physical machine, nevertheless. Virtual disks are basically parts of the actual disks, and virtual devices are made by dividing the physical hardware.

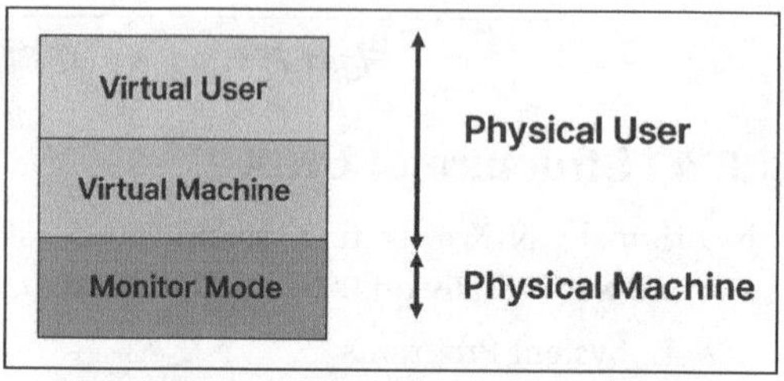

Fig 1.9: Boundary between Physical user and Physical machine

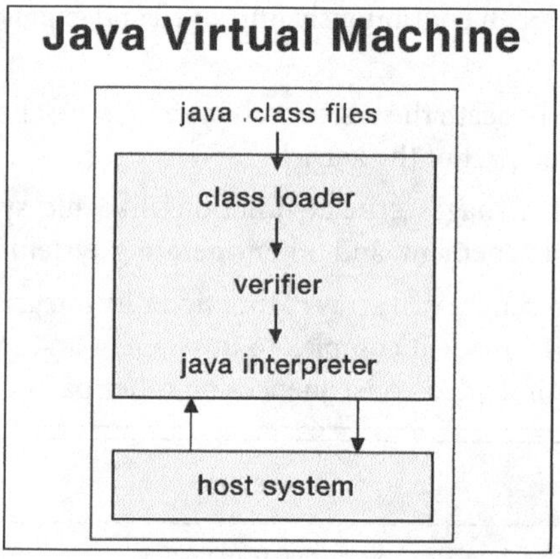

Fig. 1.10: JVM Java Virtual Machine

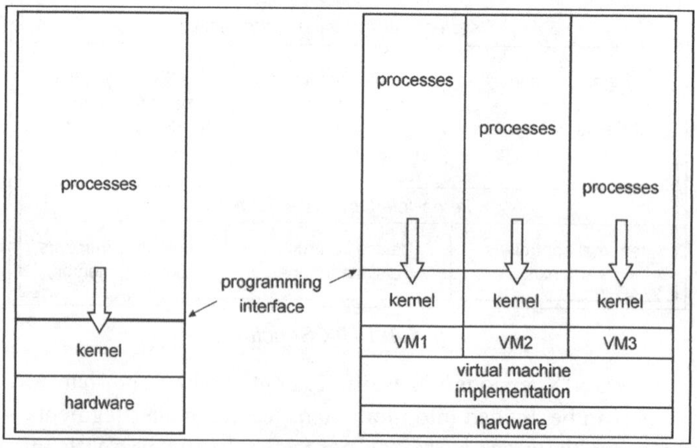

Fig. 1.11: Process Level View of VM

1.3 SYSTEM COMPONENTS

An operating system can be developed as a large and intricate system by breaking it down into smaller, more manageable parts. Each part should be a clearly defined segment of the system, with precisely specified inputs, outputs, and functions. While not all systems follow the same structure, many contemporary operating systems aim to support similar types of system components:

- Process Management
- Main Memory Management
- File Management
- I/O System Management
- Secondary Management
- Networking
- Protection System
- Command-Interpreter System

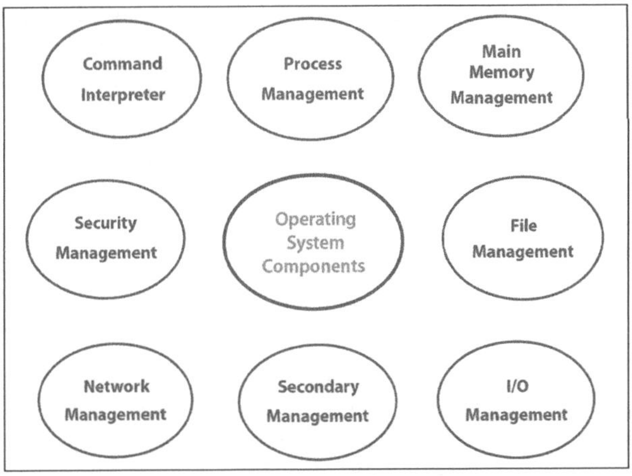

Fig. 1.12: Components of OS

Process Management

In addition to user programs, the operating system also manages system programs including file servers, printer spoolers, and name servers. A procedure represents each of these tasks. A program does not qualify as a process in and of itself; it only does so when it is in execution.

For example:

- A batch job is a process.
- A time-shared user program is a process.
- A system task, like spooling output to a printer, is a process.

Take an example– Spooling output to a printer is an example of a system task. The same program can be run concurrently by several processes. A program doesn't do anything until the CPU executes its instructions. A procedure is executed in a consecutive order. In terms of process management, the operating system's five primary roles are:

- Creation and termination of user and system processes.
- Suspension and resumption (blocking/unblocking) of processes.
- Facilitating process synchronization mechanisms.
- Enabling process communication mechanisms.
- Managing process deadlock resolution mechanisms.

Main Memory Management

One essential component of contemporary computer systems is main memory. The vast array of words or bytes that make up primary or main memory can range in size from hundreds of thousands to billions. Every word and byte has a distinct address. The CPU has immediate access to the storage provided by main memory. The CPU can directly address and access it, making it the only big storage device. A program needs to be in the main memory in order to run. Multiple programs need to be maintained in memory at the same time in order to maximize CPU utilization and enhance system reaction time.

The primary tasks of an operating system related to memory management include:

- Monitoring the current usage of memory and tracking which processes are using it.
- Deciding which processes should be loaded into memory when space becomes available.
- Allocating and deallocating memory space as required.

File Management

An essential part of an operating system, file management is crucial to how users interact with the system. Computers can store data on a variety of physical media types, including disks, CDs, and magnetic tapes. Each type of physical media has unique properties, including capacity, speed, data transfer rate, and access mechanisms. The OS offers a uniform logical picture of data storage to make user interaction easier. A file abstracts the physical properties of the storage medium and functions as a logical storage unit. Usually representing programs (both source and object forms) or data, it is a grouping of related items that has been established by its developer. The following file management-related duties are under the purview of the operating system:

- Creating and deleting files.
- Creating and managing directories.
- Supporting file manipulation operations.
- Mapping files onto secondary storage.
- Backing up files to stable (non-volatile) storage.

I/O System Management

The operating system abstracts the complexity of hardware devices, providing a user-friendly interface. The I/O subsystem includes:

- A memory management component takes care of buffering, caching, and spooling.
- A general device-driver interface.
- Specific drivers for different hardware devices.

Each device driver understands the specifics of the hardware it controls and manages interactions with that device.

Secondary-Storage Management

A primary function of a computer system is to run programs. These programs, along with their data, need to be loaded into main memory (primary storage) to be executed. Since primary memory is volatile and often too small to permanently store all programs and data, secondary storage is necessary to complement it. Most modern systems use disk drives as the main medium for online storage, holding both programs and data. The operating system is tasked with the following activities related to secondary storage management:

- Free-space Management (Paging/Swapping)
- Storage Allocation: Determining the placement of data on the disk.
- Disk Scheduling: Managing the order of memory access requests for efficient processing.

Networking

A distributed system is made up of several processors that don't share clocks, memory, or peripheral devices. Every CPU has its own clock and local memory, and they can communicate with one another via high-speed buses or networks. These processors come in a range of sizes and capacities, including workstations, minicomputers, compact processors, and huge general-purpose systems. A communication network, which can be set up in various ways and functions according to a protocol, connects the processors. The network may be partially or completely connected. Routing, connection tactics, and resolving concerns like contention and security must all be carefully considered while designing the communication network. Users can access shared resources in a distributed system, which leads to:

- Increased processing speed
- Enhanced functionality
- Greater data availability
- Improved reliability

Protection System

In a computer system that supports multiple users and allows the concurrent execution of processes, it is crucial to safeguard each process from interference by others. Protection mechanisms control access to resources such as programs, files, memory segments, and processes (CPU), ensuring that only authorized users can access them. The protection system must:

- Differentiate between legitimate and unauthorized access.
- Define and apply the appropriate access controls.
- Ensure enforcement of these controls.

Command Interpreter System

The command interpreter is an essential part of the operating system, it acts as an interface between the user and the system. It takes user commands and carries them out, typically by transforming them into system calls. Processing and executing each command as directed by the user is the command interpreter's main duty. Typical commands that the interpreter handles include:

- Creating and managing processes
- Handling input and output operations
- Managing secondary storage
- Managing main memory
- Accessing the file system
- Implementing protection mechanisms
- Managing networking tasks

1.4 OPERATING SYSTEM SERVICES

An operating system creates the environment necessary for executing programs and offers a variety of services to both the programs and their users. While specific services can differ across operating systems, there are common categories. These services are designed to make the development and execution of programs more convenient for the programmer. Some of the typical OS services include:

1. Program Execution
2. Input/ Output Operations
3. File System Management
4. Communication
5. Error Detection
6. Resource Allocation
7. Accounting
8. Protection and Security

1. Program Execution

The operating system must be capable of loading and executing a program. Program execution should be able to end either normally or with an error message.

2. I/O Operations

Input/output (I/O) procedures, which may involve files or I/O devices, may be necessary for a functioning program. Special functions might be needed for some devices (e.g., rewinding a tape drive or clearing a CRT screen). To ensure system integrity and efficiency, the operating system typically manages I/O operations, as users cannot directly execute them.

3. File System Manipulation

Programs often need to perform various file operations such as reading, writing, creating, deleting, and searching for files and directories. The operating system provides the necessary functionality for manipulating files, including managing file permissions.

4. Communication

Information sharing between processes may be necessary. There are two methods of communication: through a network between processes on various computers or between processes on the same computer. Shared memory and message forwarding, in which the operating system helps processes exchange information, are two ways to accomplish communication.

5. Error Detection

The operating system must continuously monitor for errors. These errors can occur in:

1. Hardware (e.g., memory errors or power failures)
2. I/O devices (e.g., tape errors, connection issues, or printer failures)
3. User programs (e.g., arithmetic overflow or illegal memory access)

The operating system must respond to these errors to ensure proper system functioning. Debugging tools can help users and developers troubleshoot effectively.

6. Resource Allocation

When multiple users or processes are running simultaneously, the operating system must allocate resources efficiently. It manages resources such as CPU cycles, memory, and storage. Specific resource allocation mechanisms exist for different types of resources.

7. Accounting

To track the usage of system resources, the operating system maintains records of which users are consuming resources. This can be used for billing or simply to gather usage statistics.

8. Protection & Security

In systems with multiple users, access to resources must be controlled. Protection ensures that one process cannot interfere with another or with the operating system itself. Security refers to measures taken to protect the system from unauthorized access and external threats. This involves user authentication and safeguarding against malicious access attempts.

1.5 SYSTEM CALLS

When developing a simple program to copy data from one file to another, system calls play a crucial role. The program first needs the names of two files:

- Input File – The file from which data is read.
- Output File – The file where the copied data is stored.

The method of specifying file names depends on the operating system:

I. In an **interactive system**, the program can prompt the user to enter the file names using system calls for displaying messages and reading user input.

II. In **GUI-based systems**, file selection can be done through menus or dialog boxes

- After obtaining the file names, the software needs to:
- Open the input file – If the file does not exist or has restricted access, an error message is displayed, and the program may terminate.

- Create the output file – If a file with the same name already exists, the system may:
- Overwrite the file.
- Delete the existing file.
- Prompt the user for action.
- Reading and Writing Data

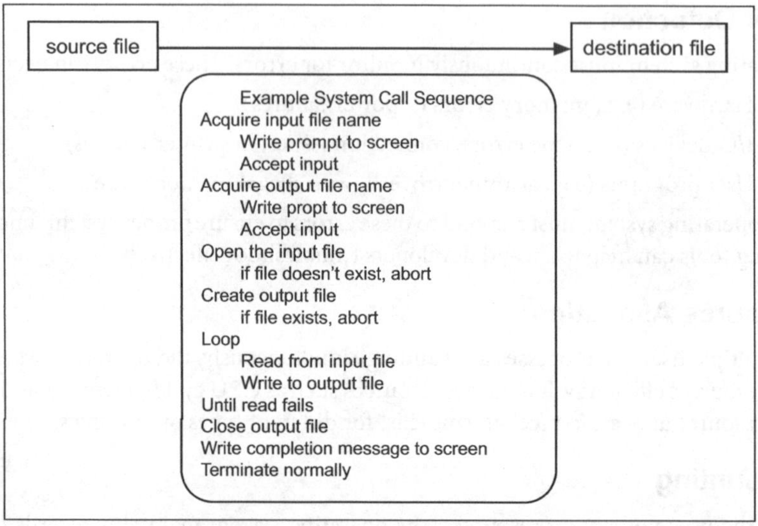

Fig. 1.13: *File Duplication system calls*

After setting up both files, the program enters a loop where it:

- Reads data from the input file (using a system call).
- Writes data to the output file (another system call).
- Handles errors such as:
  - End of file reached.
  - Hardware failures (e.g., disk errors).
  - Output issues (e.g., insufficient disk space or printer out of paper).
  - Closing Files and Program Termination

Once the copying process is complete, the program:

- Closes both files using system calls.
- Displays a confirmation message on the console.
- Terminates execution properly using a final system call.

Even a basic file-copying program requires multiple system calls, demonstrating the crucial role of the operating system in handling file management operations.

System calls provide the mechanism for user programs to interact with the operating system. These calls are typically available through assembly language instructions, though some systems allow calling system functions from high-level languages like C, C++, or Perl. System calls are used for various tasks, such as reading or writing files, managing memory, or interacting with I/O devices.

System calls can be categorized into five broad types:

1. Process Control
2. File Management
3. Device Management
4. Information Maintenance
5. Communication

System calls allow programs to request operating system services and interact with system resources. These calls use various methods to pass parameters between the user program and the OS, such as passing parameters through registers, using memory tables, or pushing parameters onto a stack.

System calls allow programs to interact with the operating system. Depending on the type and amount of information required, there are different methods to pass parameters to system calls. The choice of method depends on factors like the number of parameters and the system's design. Here are the three common approaches:

The simplest method where parameters are directly placed in CPU registers. Suitable for cases where there are a few parameters.

The address of the table is passed to the system call through a register, used when there are too many parameters to fit in registers.

The operating system pops the parameters off the stack during the system call execution.

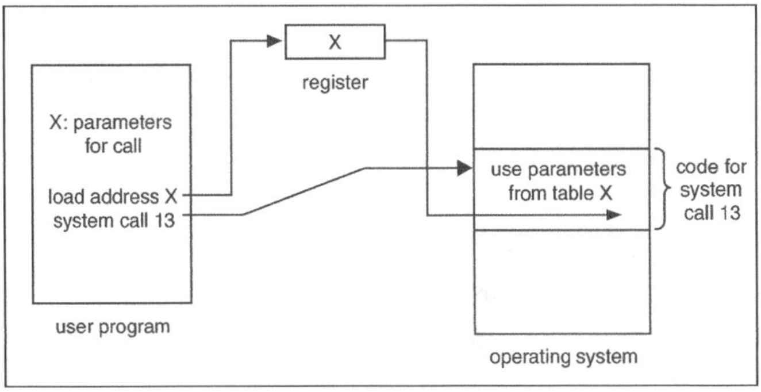

***Fig. 1.14:** Parameter passing Mechanism*

Types of System Calls

System calls are commonly categorized into five major types based on their functionality. These categories help in organizing how programs interact with the operating system and hardware. The five categories are:

1. Process Control

System calls under Process Control manage processes in the system, allowing the operating system to create, manage, and terminate processes.

Typical operations in this category include:

- Loading and executing processes

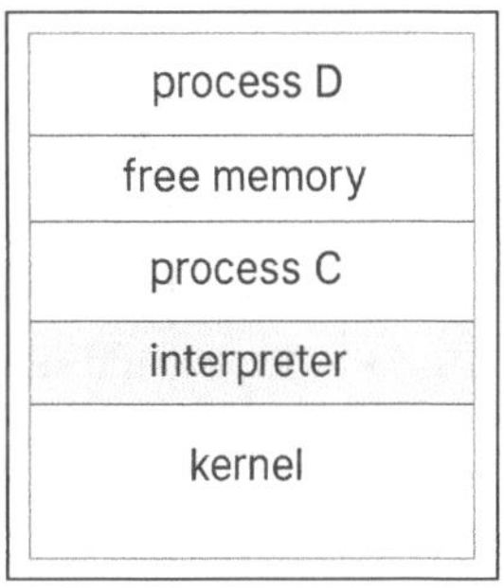

***Fig 1.15:** UNIX Running Multiple Programs*

- Aborting or terminating a process
- Creating and terminating processes
- Getting and setting process attributes
- Allocating and freeing memory
- Waiting for events and signalling events

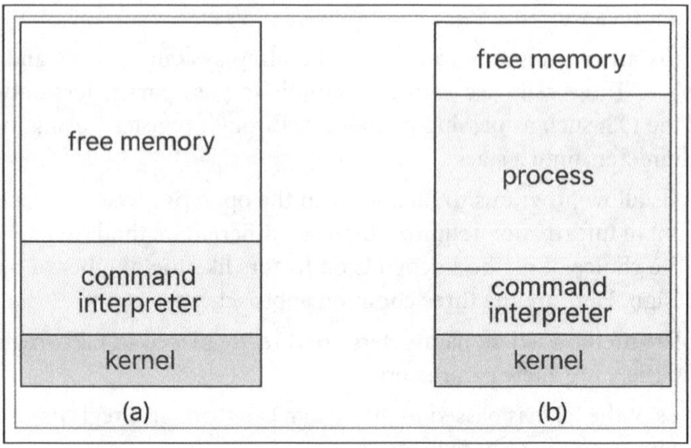

Fig. 1.16: *(a) System Startup (b) Running Program*

2. File Management

File Management system calls handle operations related to file creation, deletion, and manipulation. These allow programs to interact with files on storage devices.

Common file-related operations include:

- Creating and deleting files
- Opening and closing files
- Reading and writing data to files
- Repositioning file pointers for random access
- Getting and setting file attributes

3. Device Management

System calls in Device Management deal with controlling and interacting with hardware devices. These calls allow a program to request access to devices, manage their operations, and configure their settings.

Operations typically include:

- Requesting and releasing devices
- Reading, repositioning, and writing data to devices
- Getting and setting device attributes
- Logically attaching or detaching devices

4. Information Maintenance

Information Maintenance system calls manage and provide access to system data, time, and system configuration. These allow programs to query or modify system parameters.

Key operations include:

- Getting and setting the system date and time
- Retrieving and setting system data
- Obtaining or modifying process, file, or device attributes

5. Communication

Communication system calls facilitate inter-process communication, either within the same system or across different systems. They enable processes to share data and send/receive messages.

Communication can occur through:

- **Message Passing Model:** Where messages are sent and received between processes.
- **Shared Memory Model:** Where multiple processes access a common memory area for communication.

Common operations include:

- Creating and closing communication connections
- Sending and receiving messages
- Transferring status information
- Attaching or detaching remote devices

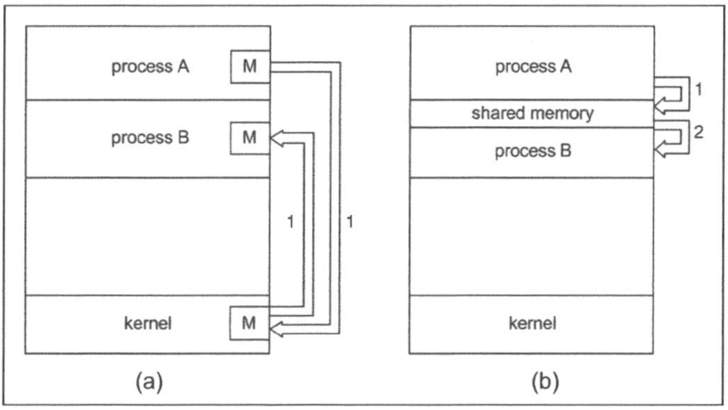

Fig. 1.17: Communication models (a) Message Passing Model (b) Shared Memory Model

1.6 RESOURCES IN THE OPERATING SYSTEM

An entity is considered a resource by the operating system if it meets certain criteria:

- **Requesting the Resource:** A process must explicitly request the resource from the OS.
- **Waiting for Allocation:** The process must pause its execution until the resource is allocated to it.

A common example of a resource is a file. Before a process can read from or write to a file, it must request the file from the operating system. If the file is not currently available, the process will wait until it becomes accessible. This concept of a resource is important in understanding how the OS manages various entities like files, memory, & hardware devices. A sequential file refers to a named, linear sequence of bytes stored in memory. Files are used to store data, and you can interact with a file by opening it through the operating system.

1.7 PROCESSES IN THE OPERATING SYSTEM

The OS runs different types of programs based on the system's configuration:

- Batch systems execute jobs.
- Time-shared systems run user programs or tasks.

Unlike just the program code, a process includes several components:

- **Program Counter (PC):** It records the program's execution point.
- **Stack:** Temporary data including function parameters, return addresses, and local variables are stored in the stack.
- **Data Section:** This contains the process's global variables.

The value in the program counter and the information in the CPU registers show the present activity of a process. Furthermore, a process may have a heap, which is RAM that is dynamically allocated while the process is running.

The process is distinct from a program. An executable file with a set of instructions saved on a disk is an example of a program, which is a passive entity. A process, on the other hand, is an active entity that requires resources while it is running, including a program counter to track the next instruction to be executed. When the operating system loads the executable file into memory, a program turns into a process.

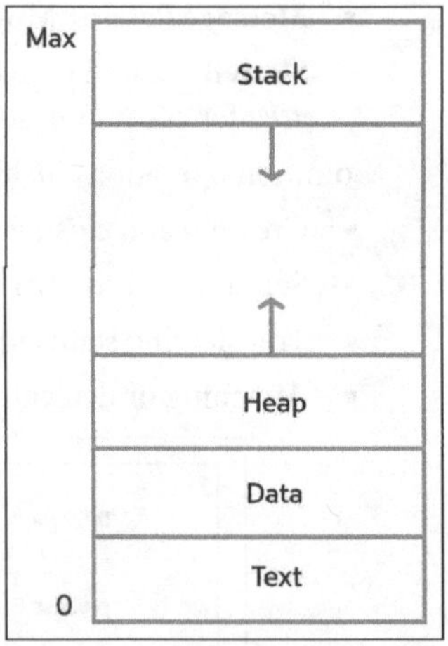

FIG 1.18: Process in Memory

Two common ways to load an executable file into memory are:

- Double-clicking the file's icon.
- Typing the file's name in the command line (e.g., prog.exe or a).

Each time a program is run, it is treated as a separate process. For example, several users may run different instances of the same application, such as a mail program, or a single user may run multiple instances of a web browser. Each of these instances is a separate process. While they share the same program code (text section), their data, heap, and stack sections are different.

Additionally, a process can create other processes while it is running.

1.8 THREADS

Sometimes referred to as a lightweight process, a thread is part of a process, which is considered a heavyweight process. A thread has the following components:

- Thread ID
- Program counter
- Register set
- Stack

In general, a process is linked to a single thread of execution. For instance, a word processor can only execute one task at a time since only one thread may run at a time. This implies that typing and using a spell checker cannot be done at the same time.

Historically, processes have only used one thread of execution. Nonetheless, contemporary operating systems have developed to accommodate multi-threaded processes. This enables a process to manage several jobs at once.

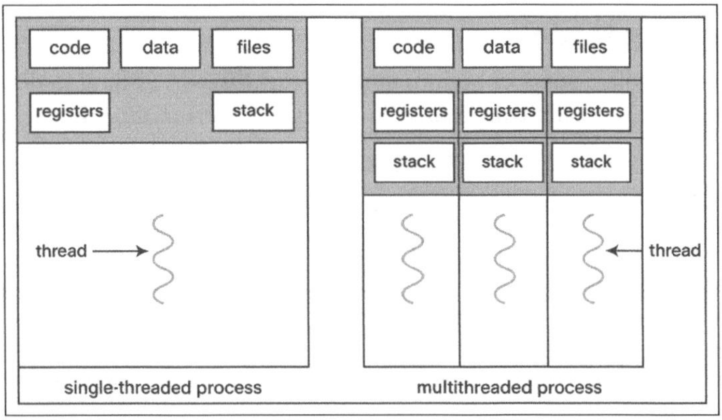

Fig. 1.19: Processes involving Single Thread and Multi Thread

The operating system plays a crucial role in managing processes and threads, including:

- Creating and deleting user and system processes.
- Scheduling processes for execution.
- Providing synchronization mechanisms for processes.
- Enabling communication between processes.
- Handling deadlock situations involving processes.

Benefits of Multithreading

Multithreading in programming provides several key benefits, which can be summarized in four major categories:

Responsiveness

Multi-threading enables interactive programs to maintain responsiveness even when doing a lengthy operation or when a portion of the program is stalled. A multi-threaded web browser, for example, could allow the user to continue engaging with the software without any delays by using one thread to handle user interactions while another thread loads an image.

Resource Sharing

Threads within a process share the memory and resources of the parent process by default. This sharing of resources allows an application to have multiple threads of execution running within the same address space, providing the advantage of resource efficiency.

Kernel Threads

The operating system directly supports and controls kernel threads, with the kernel handling thread creation, scheduling, and management in the kernel space. The benefit of kernel threads is that, in the event that a user thread is blocked, the kernel can schedule another one, even though they are more time-consuming to construct and maintain. Additionally, kernel threads can be executed on several processors in multiprocessor settings. Numerous contemporary operating systems, including Solaris 2, Windows 2000, Windows NT, and others, support kernel threads.

Multi-threading Models

Operating systems often support both user and kernel threads, leading to different multi-threading models. These models define how user and kernel threads are mapped and managed:

1. Many-to-One Model

The thread management occurs entirely in user space, which makes it efficient. However, if one thread blocks, the entire process blocks as well. Additionally, this model does not allow threads to run concurrently on multiprocessors. The Green threads library used in Solaris 2 is an example of this model.

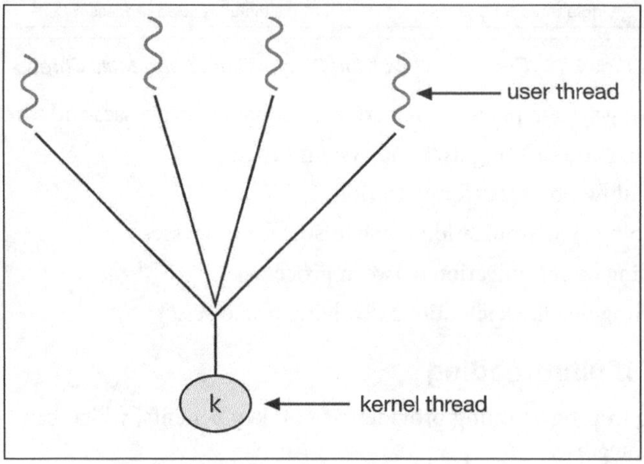

Fig. 1.20: *Many to One Model*

2. One-to-One Model

This model maps each user thread to a kernel thread, offering more concurrency. If a thread performs a blocking system call, other threads can continue executing. Additionally, this model allows threads to run in parallel on multiprocessors. However, the overhead of creating kernel threads can be a disadvantage, and the system may limit the number of threads. Operating systems like Linux and Windows use this model.

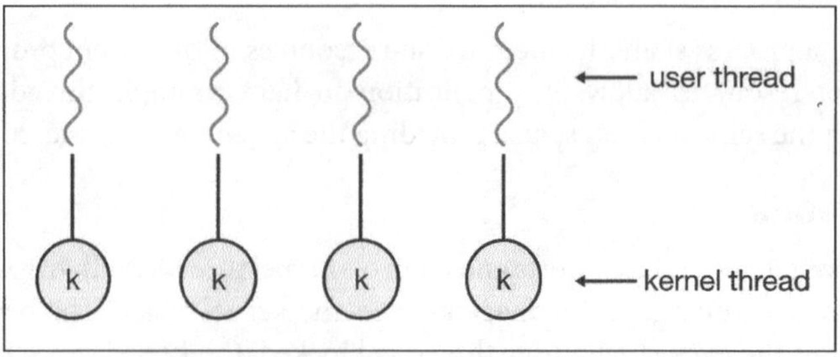

Fig. 1.21: *One to One Model*

3. Many-to-Many Model

This model allows many user-level threads to be multiplexed onto a smaller or equal number of kernel threads. The kernel threads can run in parallel, especially on multiprocessor systems, and when a thread blocks, another thread can be scheduled for execution. Operating systems such as Solaris 2, IRIX, and HP-UX support this model.

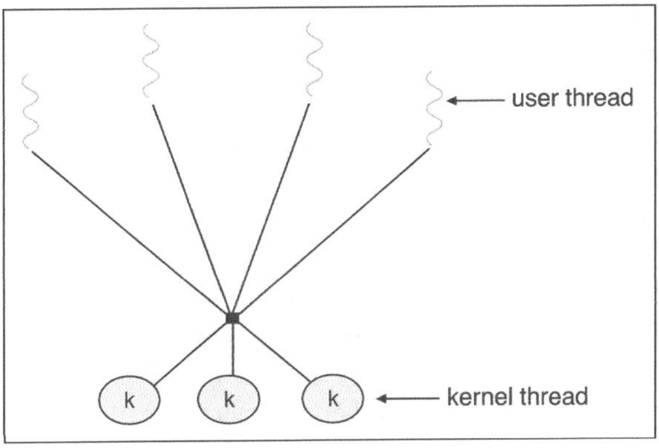

Fig. 1.22: Many to Many Model

Although processes and threads share similarities, they differ in significant ways:

Similarities

Both threads and processes share the CPU and execute sequentially within a given process or program. Both can create child processes or threads. When one thread or process is blocked, another can execute.

Differences

Processes are independent entities, while threads within a process are not.

Threads within a process are designed to cooperate, whereas processes may not be designed to interact with one another, especially if they come from different users.

1.9 OBJECTS IN OBJECT-ORIENTED PROGRAMMING

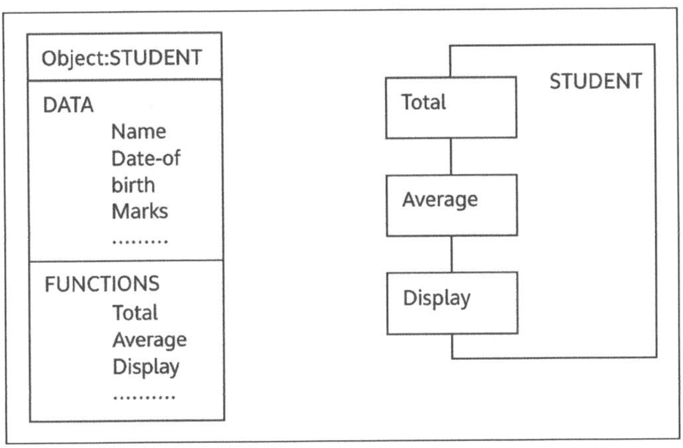

Fig. 1.23: Two ways of representing an object

In object-oriented programming (OOP), objects are runtime entities that can represent real-world items, such as a person, a bank account, or a table of data. These objects interact with one another by sending messages, with each object containing both data and code to manipulate that data. Objects can communicate without needing to know the specifics of each other's data or code, only the type of message they accept and the response they return.

1.10 DEVICE MANAGEMENT

The operating system manages hardware devices through their respective drivers. Key activities in device management include:

- Tracking all devices using the I/O controller.
- Providing a uniform interface to access devices with differing physical characteristics. Efficiently allocating and deallocating devices as needed.
- Deciding which process gets access to which device and for how long. Optimizing the performance of individual devices.
- Approaches to Device Management Direct I/O: Involves explicitly transferring data to and from the device controller's registers, sometimes with polling (checking the device's status) or interrupts (to signal completion).
- Memory-Mapped I/O: The device is treated as a range of memory locations, simplifying the interface. This can also be implemented with polling or interrupts.

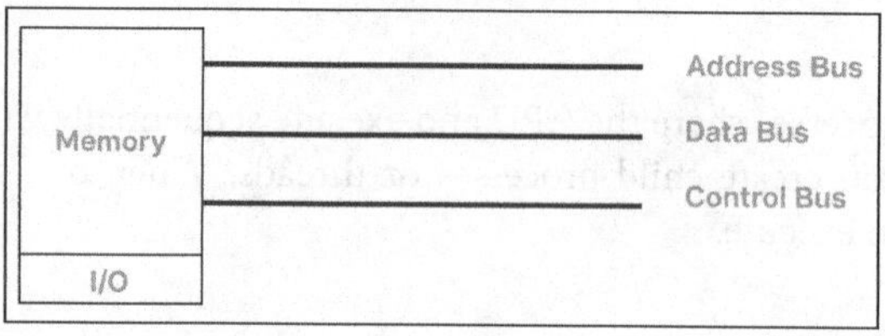

Fig. 1.24

1.11 I/O SYSTEM ORGANIZATION

In an I/O system, an application interacts with a device by sending commands and transferring data through the device management system, which includes the device driver. The device driver acts as an intermediary, facilitating communication between the application and the hardware.

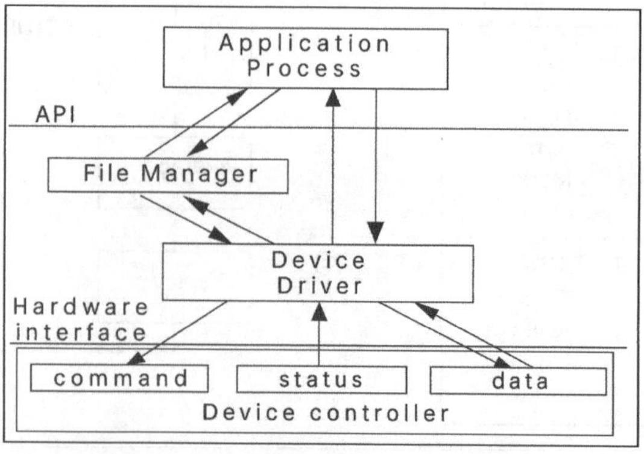

Fig. 1.25: I/O System Organization

Responsibilities of a device driver include:

- Implementing Communication APIs that provide an abstraction of the device's functionality, making it easier for software to interact with hardware without needing to understand the low-level details.
- Providing Device-Specific Operations to fulfil the functions defined by the API. These operations ensure the API works with the unique features of the specific hardware device.
- The API should be consistent across different device drivers, minimizing the amount of device-specific information an application developer needs to know. This enables easier integration of devices into software applications, regardless of the underlying hardware.

Since each device controller is unique to its device, the device driver must handle device-specific tasks, such as:

- Sending the right commands to the controller to ensure the device operates as expected.
- Interpreting the controller's status register (CSR) to determine the device's current state, like whether it's ready to perform an operation or has encountered an error.
- Managing data transfers to and from the device's controller data registers, ensuring accurate communication for proper device operation.

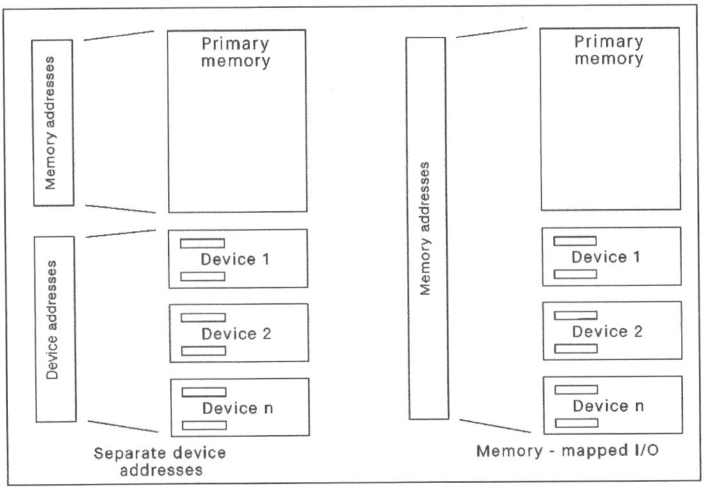

***Fig. 1.26:** Direct I/O vs. Memory Mapped I/O*

I/O With Polling

In direct I/O polling, the coordination between software and hardware is necessary to complete I/O operations effectively. The device driver manages this coordination, where the device manager continuously checks the status flags (such as busy or done flags) to monitor the completion of an operation. In this method, the CPU initiates the I/O process and then repeatedly checks the device's Control and Status Register (CSR) to determine when the operation has finished. However, this approach leads too challenges in maintaining high CPU utilization, as the CPU is tied up in continuously checking the device status instead of performing other tasks.

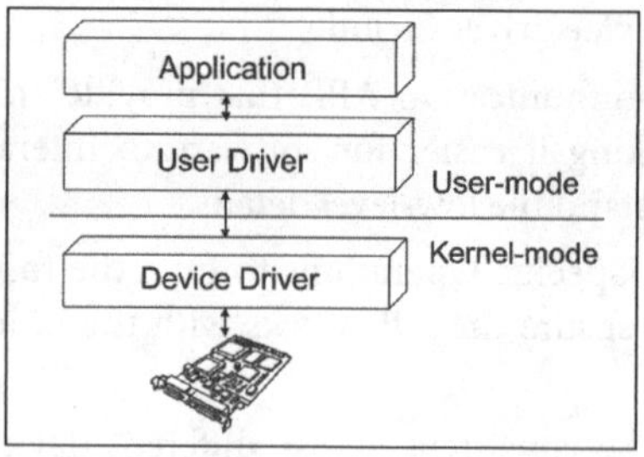

Fig. 1.27: User Mode and Kernel Mode

I/O with Polling – Read

1. The application process initiates a read request.
2. The device driver checks the Control and Status Register (CSR) to see if the device is free. If the device is in use, the driver waits until it becomes available.
3. Once the device is idle, the driver writes a read command into the controller's command register, triggering the device to start the operation.
4. The driver continuously monitors the CSR to check when the read operation has finished.
5. After the operation completes, the driver transfers the data from the controller's data registers to the user's process space in the main memory.

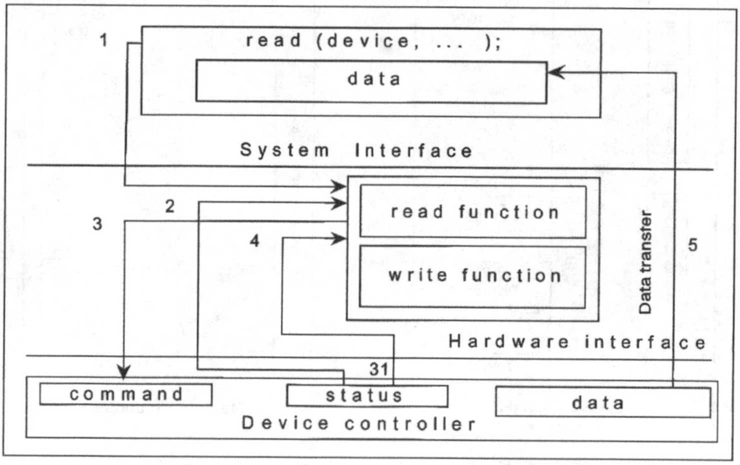

Fig. 1.28: I/O with Polling – Read

I/O with Polling – Write

The application requests a write operation:

The application initiates a request to perform a write operation to a specific device, prompting the device driver to begin the necessary steps.

The driver checks the CSR to see if the device is idle:

- The device driver queries the Control and Status Register (CSR) to check whether the device is idle or currently busy with another operation. If the device is busy, the driver will wait until the device becomes available.

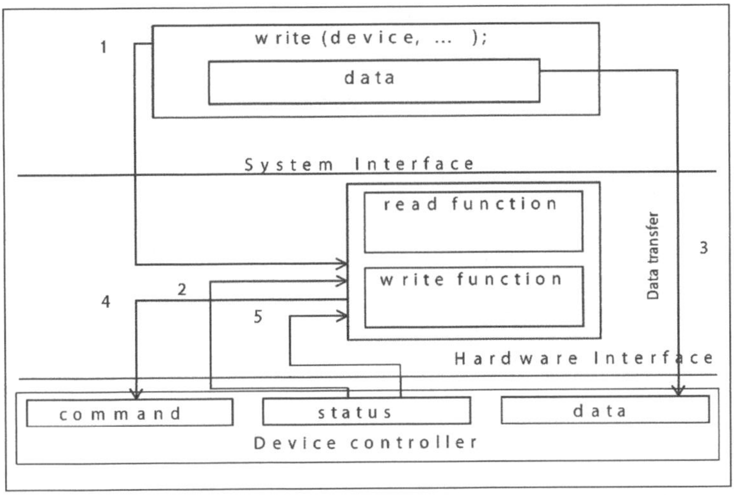

Fig. 1.29: I/O with Polling – Write

- Data is copied from user space to the controller's data registers: Once the device is idle, the driver transfers the data from the application's user space memory to the device's data registers, which hold the data temporarily before the device processes it.
- The driver issues a command to the device to start the operation: After the data is transferred, the driver writes an output command into the command register of the device, signalling it to begin the operation (such as writing data to a disk or sending it over a network).
- The driver repeatedly checks the CSR to monitor the device's status: After issuing the command, the driver continuously polls the CSR to check when the device has finished its task. The driver will keep checking until the device signals completion of the operation.

Interrupt-Driven I/O

In a multiprogramming system, polling I/O results in CPU time being wasted, as the CPU remains occupied checking for I/O completion, even when it could be performing other tasks for different processes. This issue can be mitigated by using interrupts. By using interrupts, the CPU no longer needs to constantly check if an I/O operation is complete. Instead, the device controller automatically notifies the device driver once the operation is finished, freeing up CPU resources for other tasks.

Here is how the interrupt-driven I/O process works:

- **The application requests a read operation:** The application initiates a request to read data from the device, prompting the device driver to take action.
- **The driver checks the CSR to see if the device is idle:** The device driver queries the Control and Status Register (CSR) to determine if the device is idle. If the device is busy, the driver waits until it becomes available.
- **The driver sends an input command to the controller to start the device:** Once the device is idle, the driver stores an input command in the controller's command register, triggering the device to start the operation.

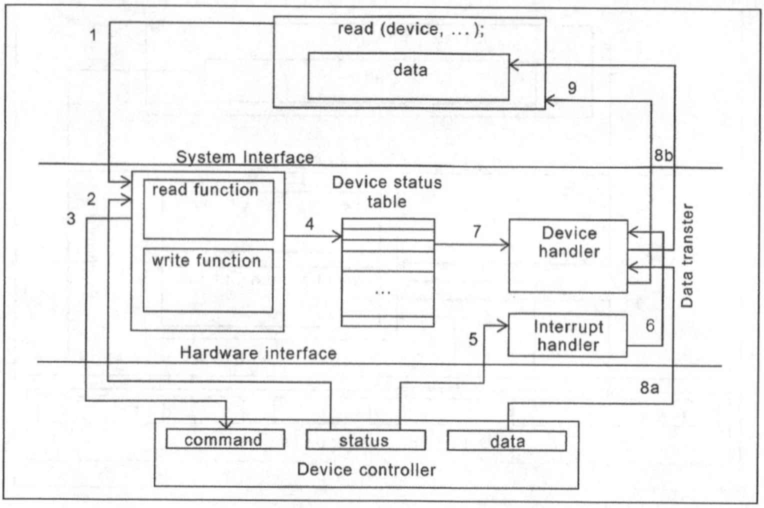

Fig. 1.30: Inerrupt-driven I/O

- **The driver saves operation details and the CPU is freed:** After issuing the command, the driver logs the relevant information about the operation in the device status table. This table includes entries for each device in the system and contains details like the return address and any special parameters needed for the I/O operation. This allows the CPU to be used by other programs while waiting for the I/O operation to complete. The scheduler then takes over, allowing the CPU to be allocated to other tasks.
- **The device completes the operation and sends an interrupt to the CPU:** Once the device has finished the operation, it interrupts the CPU, which triggers the interrupt handler to execute.
- **The interrupt handler identifies the device causing the interrupt:** The interrupt handler determines which device caused the interrupt and then jumps to the specific device handler for that device.
- **The device driver retrieves I/O status from the device status table:** The device driver accesses the device status table to retrieve information about the pending I/O operation and its status.
- **The device driver copies data to the user's space:** The driver then transfers the data from the device's data register(s) to the application's memory space, completing the I/O operation.
- **Control is returned to the application process:** After the data is copied, the device handler hands control back to the application process, using the return address stored in the device status table. A similar sequence of steps is followed for output operations.
- **Overlapping CPU Execution with Device Operation:** The software interface to an I/O device typically allows the operating system to run different processes while one process waits for I/O operations to complete, all while maintaining the serial execution order for individual processes. This ensures that when programmers use a read statement in their code, the next instruction will only execute after the read operation is finished.

For example, consider the following code:

```
read(device, "%d", x);
y = f(x);
```

Traditional I/O Methods

- **Polling Approach:** In the polling method, the CPU is responsible for transferring data between the controller's data registers and the main memory. For output operations, the device driver copies data from the application's data area to the controller, and vice versa for input operations.

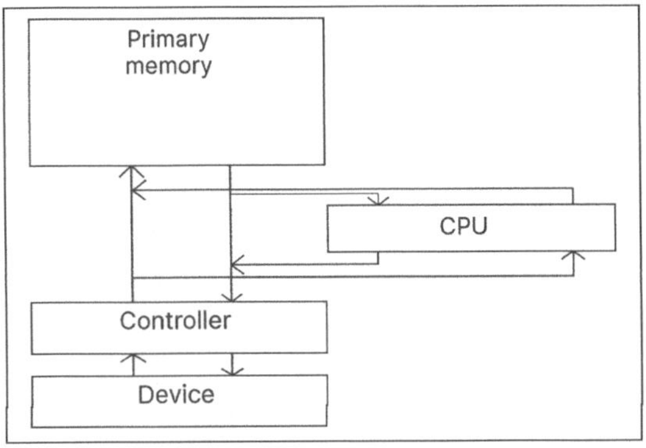

Fig. 1.31: *Traditional I/O*

- **Interrupt-Driven I/O Approach:** In this approach, the interrupt handler takes on the responsibility of managing the data transfer task when an I/O operation is completed.

DMA (Direct Memory Access)

DMA allows data to be transferred directly between the I/O device and the primary memory without involving the CPU. While the driver still initiates the I/O operation, the DMA controller manages the entire data transfer process independently of the CPU, greatly reducing the load on the processor.

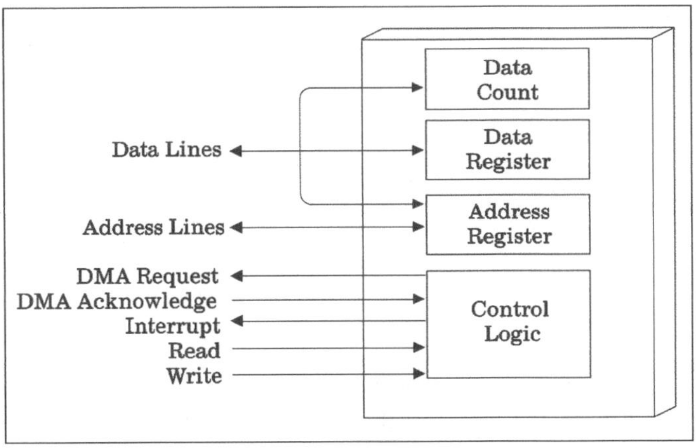

Fig. 1.32: *Typical DMA*

The DMA controller uses an address register (and sometimes additional address generation hardware) that is loaded by the device driver with a memory pointer. This pointer helps the DMA hardware identify the location of the target memory block in the primary memory for data transfer.

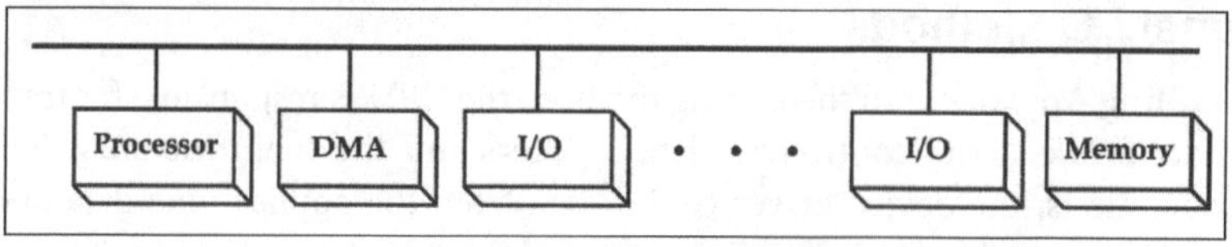

(a) Single-bus, detached DMA

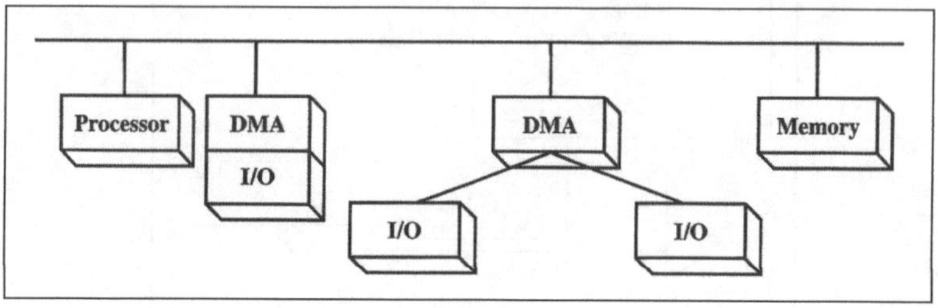

(b) Single-bus, Integrated DMA-I/O

***Fig. 1.33:** Alternative DMA Configuration*

1.12 BUFFERING

Buffering is a method used by the device manager to keep slower I/O devices active even when no immediate I/O operations are requested by a process. Input buffering involves pre-loading data into primary memory before the process actually needs it. Output buffering, on the other hand, involves temporarily storing data in memory and then transferring it to the device while the process continues executing.

- **Hardware-Level Buffering:** Consider a basic character device controller that reads a single byte from a modem during each input operation.

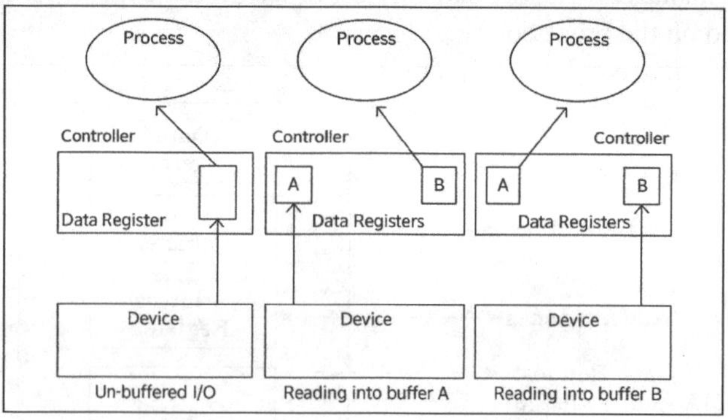

***Fig. 1.34:** Hardware-Level Buffering*

- **Normal Operation:** When a read is requested, the driver sends a read command to the controller. The controller then directs the device to place the next character into its one-byte data register. The process that requested the byte waits for the operation to finish and then retrieves the character from the data register.

- **Buffered Operation:** To reduce the wait time for the process, a hardware buffer is added to the controller. In this setup, the next character to be read is already loaded into the data register, even before the process has issued the read command. This minimizes the waiting time for the process.

Driver-Level Buffering

This technique is commonly referred to as double buffering. It involves using two buffers: one for the driver to hold data while waiting for the upper layers to read it, and the other to store data coming from the lower-level module. This method is particularly useful for block-oriented devices, where the buffers must be sufficiently large to hold a full block of data.

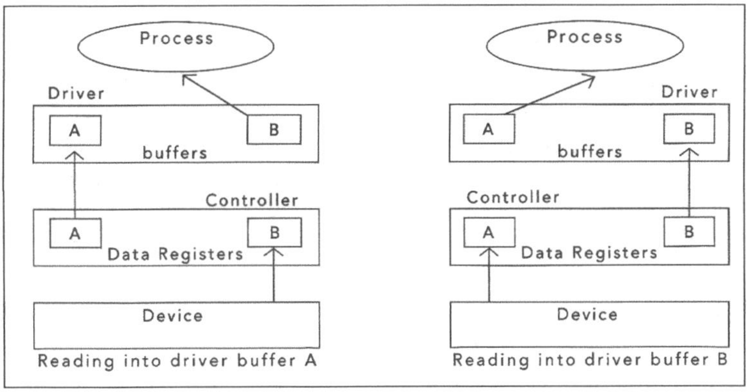

Fig. 1.35: Driver-Level Buffering

- **Using Multiple Buffers:** The concept of buffering is extended from two to n buffers. In this setup, the data producer (the controller during read operations or the CPU during write operations) writes data into buffer i, while the data consumer (the CPU during read operations or the controller during write operations) reads data from buffer j. In this configuration, buffers j+1 to n-1 and 0 to i-1 are already filled. This technique is referred to as circular buffering.

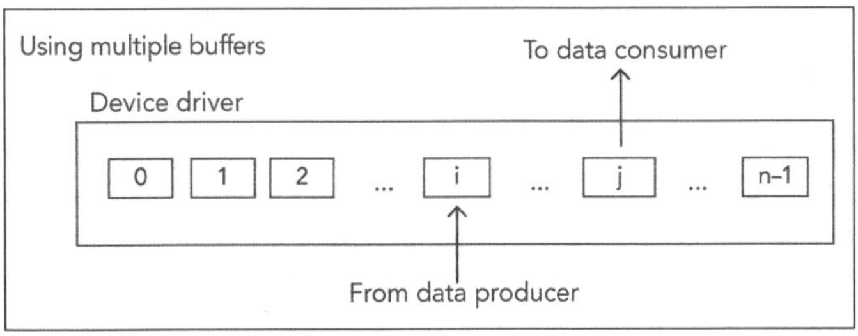

Fig. 1.36: Using Multiple Buffers

- **Device Driver:** A device driver is a software component that manages and controls a specific type of hardware connected to the computer. It provides a standardized interface to the hardware, allowing the operating system to interact with the device without needing to know the device's specific details. Communication between the driver and the device occurs through a bus or communication subsystem.

Key Responsibilities

- **Initialize Devices:** Set up and configure devices when they are first used.
- **Interpret Commands:** Translate and handle instructions from the operating system for the device.
- **Manage Data Transfers:** Oversee the transfer of data between the device and the system.
- **Handle Interrupts:** Respond to interrupts from the device to process urgent operations.
- **Ensure Data Integrity:** Protect the consistency of both the driver and kernel data structures during operations.

Device Driver Interface

Every operating system defines its own architecture for device management, and these designs vary across different systems. There isn't a universal structure for device management. However, each operating system provides two main interfaces for interacting with the device manager: The Driver API. The Interface between the driver and the operating system kernel Driver API The Driver API offers a set of functions that programmers can use to manage devices, such as communication devices or storage devices. The device manager has several responsibilities when managing devices:

- **Tracking Device State:** It must monitor the device's status, noting when it is idle, in use, and which process is using it.
- **Maintaining the Device Status Table:** The device manager must keep the device status table up to date.
- **Device Descriptors:** It may also maintain a device descriptor, which stores additional details about the device.

The API includes the following key functions:

Open/Close Functions

- **Open:** Allocates the device and initializes necessary tables and resources for its use.
- **Close:** Releases dynamic table entries and frees the device for other use.

Read/Write Functions

These functions allow the programmer to perform read or write operations on the device. Since not all devices behave the same, these operations are divided into device classes for consistency: Character Devices or Block Devices Sequential Devices or Random Access Devices.

- **IOCtl Function:** This function allows the programmer to implement device-specific commands and functions that aren't covered by the basic read/write operations.

The Driver-Kernel Interface

Device drivers need to execute privileged instructions when interacting with hardware, which means they must run as part of the operating system rather than as user programs.

Additionally, drivers must have the capability to read and write data across the address spaces of different processes, as the same driver may be used by multiple processes.

There are two main approaches to handling device drivers:

1. Traditional Approach

In the past, the device driver was tightly integrated with the operating system. To add a new driver, the entire operating system needed to be recompiled, which was a cumbersome process.

2. Modern Approach

Today, operating systems allow the installation of new drivers without requiring a full recompilation. This is achieved through reconfigurable device drivers, where the OS dynamically links the OS code to the driver functions.

A reconfigurable driver must follow a fixed, standardized API.

The kernel must provide an interface that enables the device driver to allocate and deallocate memory for buffers, manipulate kernel tables, and perform other essential tasks.

Reconfigurable Device Driver

The operating system utilizes an indirect reference table to access various driver entry points, which are determined by the device identifier and the function name. This table is populated with the correct values when the device driver is loaded, either during Plug and Play (PnP) device detection or at boot time. When a process makes a system call, the kernel forwards the call to the appropriate device driver through this indirect reference table.

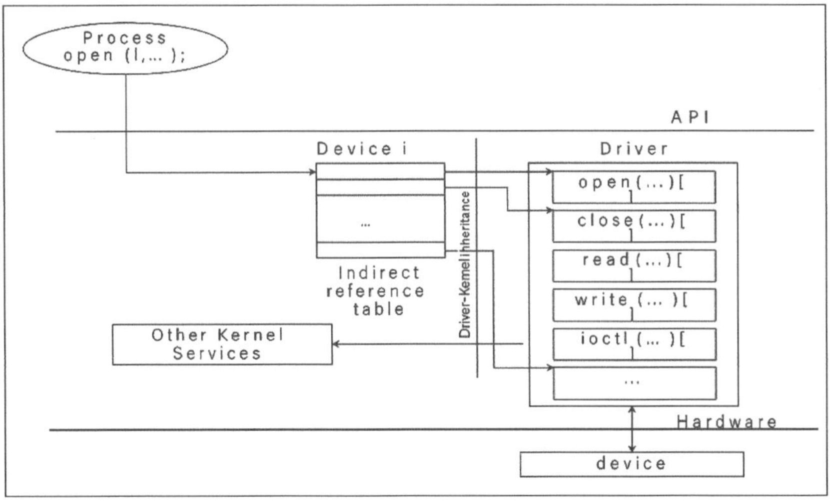

Fig. 1.37: Reconfiguration Device Drivers

UNIT 2

Introduction to Processes

INTRODUCTION

The sole program that could execute on an early computer system had total control over the machine and access to all of its resources. On the other hand, because contemporary computer systems can execute numerous programs at once, resource management needs to be more disciplined.

The idea of a "process" was developed to handle this added complexity. A program that is presently running is basically what a process is. A process needs to follow a sequential path of execution in order to function, guaranteeing that its duties are completed in a systematic way. A process requires specific resources, including CPU time, memory, files, and I/O devices, to carry out its tasks.When the process is created or continues to run, these resources are assigned to it. One definition of a process is the basic unit of labor that occurs within a system.

A system consists of a number of processes. While some of these processes are user processes running application code, others are operating system processes running system-level code. Multi-threaded processes are now supported by modern operating systems, although early systems usually used processes with a single thread of activity. A process is the fundamental unit of work in a contemporary time-sharing system, and the operating system closely monitors how it is carried out. Operating systems have become more complicated as a result of their evolution, and users now demand them to accomplish a wide range of activities. An operating system manages system duties that are better handled outside the kernel, even if its main function is to run user programs.

Therefore, a computer system is made up of a variety of processes, some of which run user programs and others of which execute operating system code.

2.1 PROCESSES

A program that is in the execution phase, where its execution is dictated by particular priorities or algorithms, or follows a sequential order, can be thought of as a process. A process is, in essence, a reality that symbolizes the primary function given to a system. Typically, this procedure is broken down into four essential parts.

- Heap
- Mound
- Data
- Text

Each of these sections plays a distinct part in the operation of a process.

2.2 PROCESS CONCEPTS

One of the most frequent questions when talking about operating systems is how to describe the different CPU processes. The word "job" is used to refer to tasks in a batch system, while "task" or "user program" is frequently used to refer to the activities being carried out in a time-sharing system.

Multiple programs, such as a word processor, web browser, or email client, can be executed simultaneously by a person even on single-user platforms like Microsoft Windows. Memory management is one example of an internal activity that the operating system may still need to handle even if just one program is running at once.

All of these different actions are commonly referred to as processes because of their similarities. "Process" and "job" are frequently used interchangeably. Even though the word "process" is used more frequently now, a large portion of operating system theory and nomenclature dates back to a period when task processing was the main focus. Thus, even though "process" has essentially supplanted "job" in many instances, it is crucial to keep using terms like "job scheduling," which are still part of the commonly used language.

The Process

Depending on the type of system, an operating system can run several kinds of programs: These programs are called jobs in a batch system. They are referred to as user programs or tasks in a time-shared system.

A program that is currently running is referred to as a process. It contains a number of elements necessary for the program's operation in addition to the code (also known as the text portion), such as:

- **Program Counter:** This maintains the execution point's current value.
- **Program Stack:** This holds temporary information, including local variables, return addresses, and function parameters.
- **Data Section:** Contains global variables.

Furthermore, memory that is dynamically allocated during the process's runtime is known as a *heap*. Together, these components guarantee that the procedure runs smoothly.

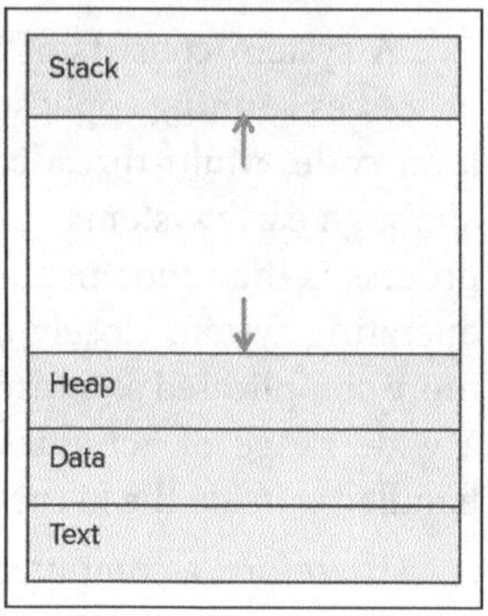

Fig. 2.1: The Process

- **Stack:** Local variables, return addresses, and method or function parameters are examples of temporary data stored in the process stack.
- **Heap:** This is the memory dynamically allocated to a process during its execution.
- **Text:** This section shows the current state of the process, including the contents of the processor's registers and the value of the program counter.

It's crucial to remember that a program is not a process in and of itself. A program is a passive entity, usually a file (also known as an executable file) that contains instructions saved on disk. A process, on the other hand, is an active entity that is identified by its resources and a program counter that indicates the next instruction to be executed. When an executable file is put into memory and starts running, a program is referred to as a process.

Process State/Process Life Cycle

A process goes through several phases while it is running. There is no standard naming scheme for the various stages, and their names can differ throughout operating systems. Generally speaking, though, a process can be in any of the five states listed below at any given time:

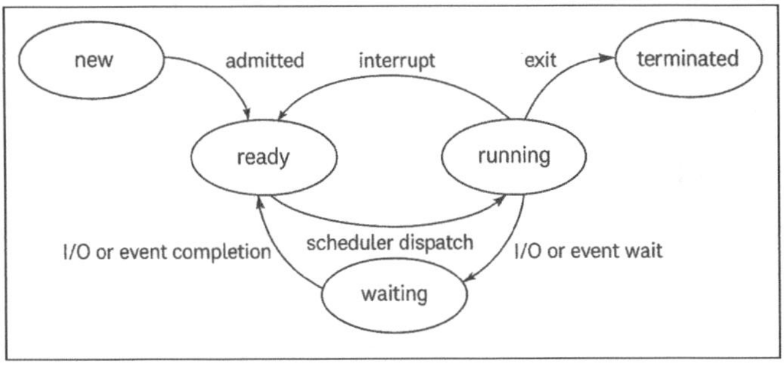

Fig. 2.2: Process life cycle

1. New/Start
2. Running
3. Waiting
4. Ready
5. Terminated

State	Description
New	The process is created but not yet admitted to execution.
Ready	The process is waiting to be assigned to the CPU.
Running	The process is currently executing on the CPU.
Blocked (Waiting)	The process is waiting for an I/O operation to complete.
Terminated	The process has completed execution or has been stopped.

Process Life Cycle Transitions

a. Process Creation (New → Ready)

When a process is created, it enters the New state.

The OS allocates necessary resources and moves it to the Ready state.

b. Process Scheduling (Ready → Running)

When the CPU is available, the scheduler selects a process from the Ready queue. The process starts executing and moves to the Running state.

c. Execution & CPU Burst (Running → Blocked/Ready)

If the process completes execution, it moves to the Terminated state. If it needs I/O (e.g., reading from a file), it moves to the Blocked state.

If a higher-priority process arrives, the OS may preempt it and move it back to Ready.

d. Process Termination (Running → Terminated)

Once a process completes its task, it releases resources and moves to the Terminated state.

Scheduling And Process Management

- Long-Term Scheduler: Controls how many processes enter the Ready queue.
- Short-Term Scheduler: Decides which process in Ready moves to Running.
- Medium-Term Scheduler: Temporarily removes processes from memory to optimize performance.

Process Control Block (PCB)

A Process Control Block (PCB) is a data structure maintained by the operating system to store information about a process. It helps the OS manage, schedule, and track the execution of processes.

Category	Description
Process ID (PID)	A unique identifier assigned to the process.
Process State	The current state of the process (New, Ready, Running, Blocked, Terminated).
Program Counter (PC)	Holds the address of the next instruction to be executed.
CPU Registers	Stores register values such as accumulator, stack, pointers and general-purpose registers.
Scheduling Information	Priority, scheduling queue pointers, and execution time details.
Memory Management Info	Base and limit registers, page tables, and segment tables for memory allocation.
I/O Status Information	List of I/O devices allocated to the process and pending I/O requests.
Accounting Information	CPU usage, execution time, and process limits for tracking system resources.

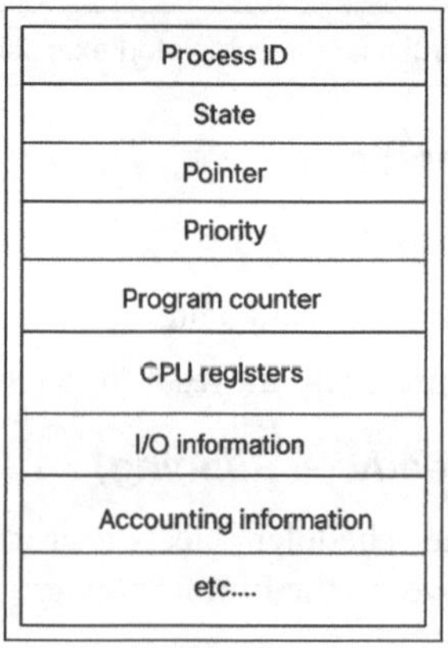

Fig. 2.3: *PCB*

The structure of the PCB can vary across different operating systems, with each OS adding specific information as needed. The PCB is maintained for the entire lifetime of a process and is deleted once the process terminates.

Diagram Showing CPU Switch Process To Process

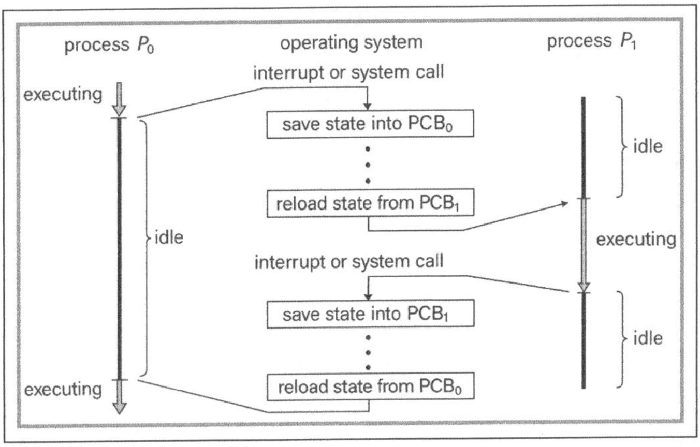

Fig. 2.4: CPU switch to process

2.3 PROCESS SCHEDULING

Only one process can be active at a time in a system with a single processor. If there are several processes running, the others have to wait for the CPU to become available so they can be rescheduled.

The purpose of multiprogramming is to keep a process active at all times so that CPU utilization is maximized.

Changing the CPU between processes often enough to allow users to interact with each program while it is running is the aim of time-sharing.

The process scheduler is in charge of choosing an available process to run on the CPU, usually from a list of ready processes, in order to accomplish these objectives.

Process Control Blocks (PCBs) in Process Scheduling Queues are entirely under the operating system's control. Every process state is kept in its own queue, and all PCBs of processes that are in the same execution state are positioned in the appropriate queue. A process's PCB is moved from its current queue to the queue for its new state when it changes states.

Process Migration Between Queues:

- Job Queue
- Ready Queue
- Device Queues

Job Queue

All of the system's processes, regardless of their present state, are contained in this queue.

Ready Queue

All of the processes that are in main memory, prepared, and awaiting execution are kept in this queue. This queue is where a newly generated process is originally put.

Device Queue

Because they are awaiting access to an I/O device, the processes in these queues are stalled.

To handle each queue, the operating system may use a variety of scheduling policies, including FIFO, Round Robin, and Priority. Only one process can occupy the running state per processor core, and the OS scheduler controls how processes switch between the ready and running queues.

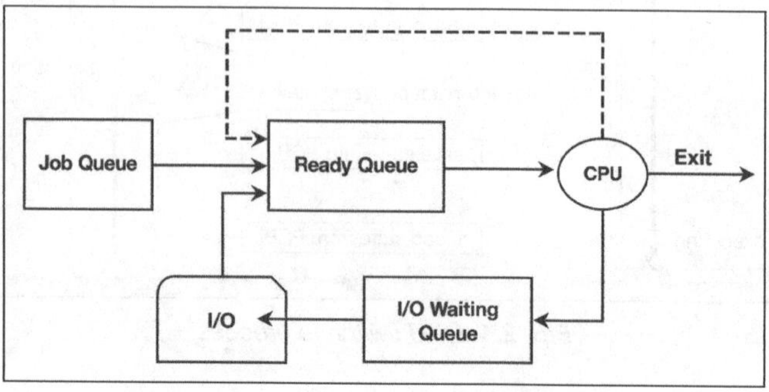

Fig. 2.5: Process Scheduling Queues

Two State Process Model

The two-state process model consists of two main states:

Running and Non-Running

These states are described as follows:

Running

When a new process is created, it comes into the system in the condition of running, actively carrying out its commands.

Non-Running

In a queue, pending their turn to execute, are processes that are not executing at the moment. A pointer to a particular process is contained in each item of this queue. A linked list structure is usually used to implement the queue.

Queuing Diagram Representation for Process Scheduling

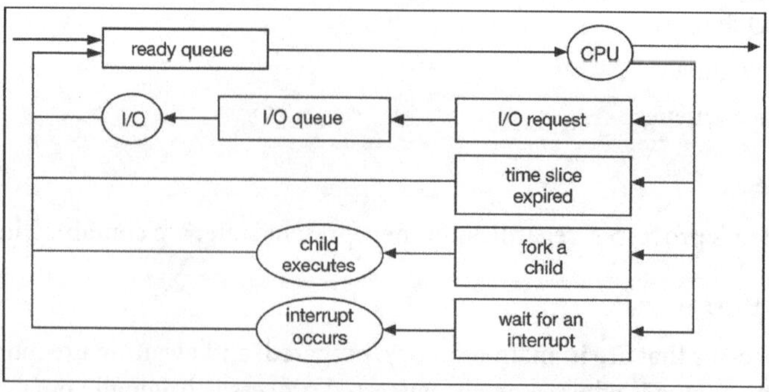

Fig. 2.6: Queuing Diagram

In the process scheduling system, each **rectangular box** represents a queue. There are two main types of queues:

- The **Ready Queue**
- A set of **Device Queues**

The circles represent the resources that service these queues, and the arrows indicate the flow of processes through the system.

Process Flow

New Process

When a new process is formed, it is first added to the Ready Queue and waits to be dispatched or chosen for execution.

Process Execution

A number of things might happen when the process is given the CPU and starts running: An I/O request may be sent by the process, in which case it is moved to an I/O queue. The procedure could start a new subprocess and watch for it to finish. The process could be taken out of the CPU and put back in the Ready Queue if it is pre-emptied (for instance, by an interrupt).

Returning to Ready

The process will ultimately move from the Waiting state back to the Ready state and be reinserted into the Ready Queue in the first two situations (I/O request or sub-process creation).

This loop keeps on until the process ends, at which time its PCB and resources are deallocated and it is taken out of all queues.

2.3.1 Schedulers

S.N.	Long-Term Scheduler	Short-Term Scheduler	Medium-Term Scheduler
1.	It is a job scheduler	It is a CPU scheduler	It is a process swapping scheduler.
2.	Speed is lesser than short term scheduler	Speed is fastest among other two	Speed is in between both short and long term scheduler.
3.	It controls the degree of multiprogramming	It provides lesser control over degree of multiprogramming	It reduces the degree of multiprogramming.
4.	It is almost absent of minimal in time sharing system	It is also minimal in time sharing system	It is a part of Time sharing systems.
5.	It selects processes from pool and loads them into memory for execution	It selects those processes which are ready to execute	It can re-introduce the process into memory and execution can be continued.

Schedulers are essential system software responsible for managing process scheduling in different ways. Their primary role is to choose which jobs should be entered into the system and determine which processes should be executed. There are three main types of schedulers:

1. Long-Term Scheduler
2. Short-Term Scheduler
3. Medium-Term Scheduler

1. Long-Term Scheduler

- Also appertained to as the job scheduler, the long-term scheduler is responsible for determining which programs are allowed to enter the system for processing.
- It selects processes from the line and loads them into memory for prosecution.
- The loaded processes are also available for CPU scheduling.
- The main thing of the long-term scheduler is to maintain a balanced blend of processes, similar as CPU-bound and I/ O-bound tasks.
- It also regulates the degree of multiprogramming. still, the rate at which processes are created should match the rate at which processes leave the system, if this degree remains stable.

2. Short-Term Scheduler

- Known as the CPU scheduler, the short-term scheduler's primary part is to enhance system performance grounded on predefined criteria. It's responsible for transitioning processes from the ready state to the running state.
- The CPU scheduler chooses a process from the ready line and allocates the CPU to that process.
- Short-term schedulers, also called dispatchers, are responsible for making opinions about which process should be executed next.
- These schedulers operate important faster than long-term schedulers, making frequent, quick opinions.

3. Medium-Term Scheduler

- The medium-term scheduler is associated with the switching process.
- It's responsible for removing processes from memory when demanded.
- By doing so, it helps to reduce the degree of multiprogramming. The medium-term scheduler manages processes that have been shifted out.

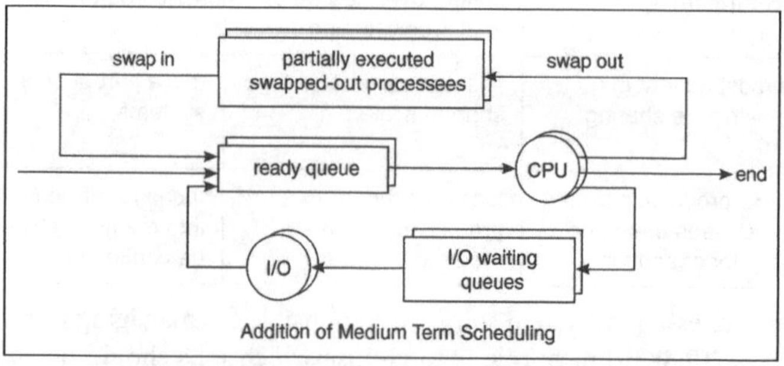

Fig. 2.7: Scheduling process

- When a handling process requests I/O operations, it may come suspended. A suspended process cannot make any farther progress.
- To free up memory for other processes, the suspended process is moved to secondary storehouse in a process called switching (or rolling out). switching helps to ameliorate the overall process blend in the system.

Context Switch

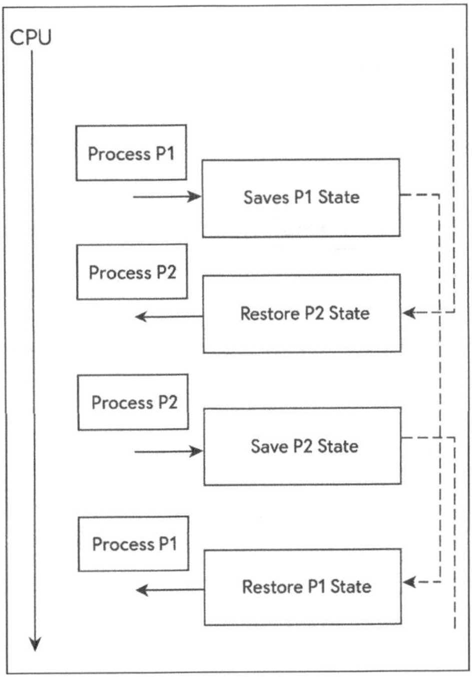

Fig. 2.8: Context switch

1. Within the procedure Control Block, a context switch is a procedure that saves and restores a CPU's state or context. This makes it possible to halt a process's execution and then pick it up where it left off.
2. Context switching enables the system to effectively handle several tasks at once by allowing numerous processes to share a single CPU.
3. A key component of multitasking operating systems is context switching, which allows the system to transition between different tasks.
4. Computational Cost: Because context switching necessitates preserving and restoring the process's state, including its register and memory contents, it is resource-intensive.
5. Some hardware systems employ numerous sets of processor registers to reduce the overhead brought on by frequent context shifts, which reduces the time required to perform the switch.

To guarantee that the process can restart properly after a context transition, the following information is saved:

1. **Program Counter:** The address of the subsequent command to be carried out.

2. **Scheduling Information:** Specifics like the priority of the procedure and additional scheduling factors.
3. **Base and Limit Register Values:** These are used to specify the process's memory limits.
4. **Currently Used Registers:** These are the registers that the process is using when it switches.
5. **Process State:** The state of the process at that moment, such as ready, waiting, or running.
6. **I/O State Information:** This refers to the state of any input/output activities that the process is carrying out.
7. **Accounting Information:** Information on how much memory or CPU time the process is using.

2.4 OPERATIONS ON PROCESSES

Processes must be dynamically launched and terminated in order to operate concurrently in a multitasking system.

- The operating system must thus provide mechanisms for starting and stopping processes.
- This section discusses how to create processes and provides examples of how to do it on Windows and UNIX platforms..

Process Creation

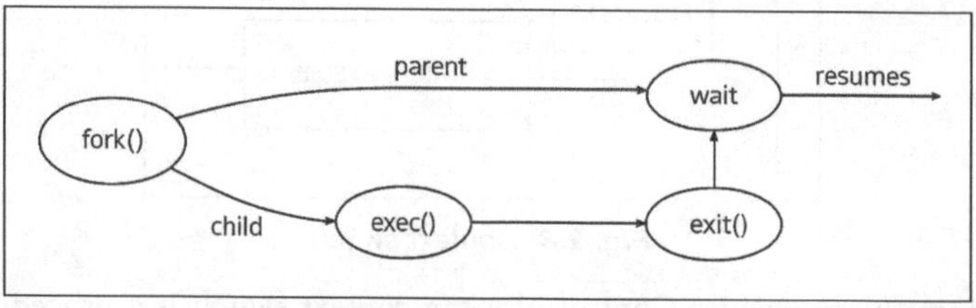

Fig. 2.9: Process creation

The parent process is in charge of producing child processes, and each of these child processes has the ability to produce further processes, forming a hierarchical structure that is sometimes called a process tree.

Resource Sharing: In some situations, a parent and children share all resources.

A portion of a parent's resources are shared by children, while certain resources are inherited by the kid.

In other situations, a parent and kid are not permitted to share any resources.

Execution: The parent and child processes are able to operate simultaneously, concurrently.

- As an alternative, the parent process can hold off on executing until the subordinate processes have finished.

The parent process is in charge of producing child processes, and each of these child processes has the ability to produce further processes, forming a hierarchical structure that is sometimes called a process tree.

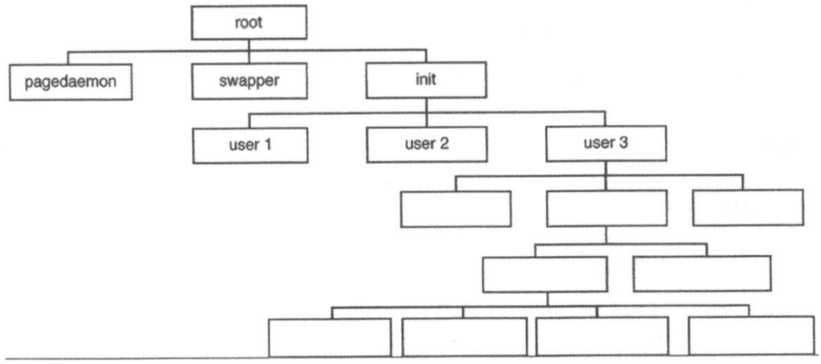

Fig. 2.10: Tree process in Unix system

Resource Sharing: In some situations, a parent and children share all resources. A portion of a parent's resources are shared by children, while certain resources are inherited by the kid. In other situations, a parent and children are not permitted to share any resources.

Execution: The parent and child processes are able to operate simultaneously, concurrently.

- As an alternative, the parent process can hold off on executing until the subordinate processes have finished.

There are two potential behaviours regarding the execution of processes when a new one is created:

- The parent process continues to run concurrently with its child processes.
- Alternatively, the parent process waits until one or more of its child processes have finished execution.

There are also two possibilities regarding the address space of the new process:

- The child process may be an exact duplicate of the parent process, meaning it inherits the parent's program and data.

2.5 COOPERATING PROCESSES

In an operating system, concurrently executing processes can be either cooperative or autonomous.

- A procedure that doesn't communicate with or is impacted by other processes in the system is said to be independent.
- A process like that doesn't share data with any other process.
- A process that has the ability to influence or be influenced by other processes within the system is said to be collaborating.

Process collaboration is crucial for a variety of reasons.

1. **Information sharing:** The system must provide concurrent access to smooth data sharing when several druggies or processes require access to the same data (participated lines, for example).
2. **Speedup of computation:** A job can be sped faster by breaking it up into smaller subtasks that run similarly, maximizing the total prosecution time.

3. **Adaptability:** A system becomes more modular and manageable when it is divided into distinct procedures or components.
4. **Practicality:** It is true that a single stoner may perform several activities simultaneously, increasing efficacy. Mechanisms for synchronization and communication are required for collaborating processes to function together.

Types of Buffers

1. Unbounded Buffer
   - There's no practical limit to the buffer size.
   - The consumer may need to stay for new particulars, but the patron can always add new particulars to the buffer.
2. Bounded Buffer
   - The buffer has a fixed size.
   - The patron will stay if the buffer is full, and the consumer will stay if the buffer is empty.

2.6 CPU SCHEDULING

- CPU scheduling, which is often caused by resource attainability (e.g., I/O operations), is the process of assigning the CPU to one task while another is momentarily interrupted in a staying state.
- This guarantees effective usage of the CPU.
- One of the processes in the ready line must be selected by the operating system to execute next when the CPU becomes idle.
- The short-term scheduler, sometimes referred to as the CPU scheduler, is in charge of making this choice.

2.6.1 CPU Scheduling Dispatcher

Another crucial component of the CPU scheduling procedure is the dispatcher. It is in charge of handing over CPU control to the process that the short-term scheduler selects. Among the dispatcher's duties is environment switching. Process state is saved and loaded. In order to renew prosecution, the CPU is directed to the appropriate location in the stoner program.

- Since the dispatcher is called each time a process transition takes place, it must function quickly.
- Dispatch quiescence is the amount of time it takes for the dispatcher to halt one activity and begin another.

2.6.2 Types of CPU Scheduling Opinions

Opinions on CPU scheduling are formed under the following four circumstances:

1. When a process changes from the running state to the staying state (for example, when a child process is waiting for its completion or when an I/O request is issued).
2. After an intrusion, for example, a process transitions from the running state to the ready state.

3. The transition of a process from the staying state to the ready state (much to the completion of I/O operations).

2.6.3 CPU Scheduling: Scheduling Criteria

- The properties of various CPU scheduling methods differ, and choosing one strategy might give one process type priority over another.
- The characteristics and performance of various scheduling algorithms should be taken into account while selecting one for a given scenario.
- CPU scheduling strategies are compared using a number of factors. These factors have a big impact on whatever algorithm is considered the best or most appropriate.

The primary criteria include:

1. **CPU Utilization:** Keeping the CPU as active as feasible is the aim. In a system that is not overloaded, CPU usage should ideally be between 40% and 90%.

   Theoretically, CPU usage may be anything between 0% and 100%.
2. **Throughput:** Throughput is the overall quantity of work done in a given length of time, or the number of processes finished per unit of time.

   Depending on the kind of procedure, it might range from 10 processes per second to 1 process per hour.
3. **Turnaround Time:** The amount of time needed to complete a procedure from the time it is submitted to the time it is finished is known as the turnaround time. Another name for this is wall-clock time.
4. **Waiting Time:** The amount of time a process waits for the CPU to execute it while it is in the ready queue is known as the waiting time. It is the period of time that a process must wait before it may start running.
5. **Average Load:** The average number of processes in the ready queue that are awaiting CPU time is known as the load average. It indicates the current load on the system.
6. **Respond Time:** The amount of time that passes between a request being submitted and the first answer being produced is known as the response time. It doesn't take the entire procedure into account; it just takes into account the time until the first answer.

2.7 SCHEDULING ALGORITHMS

CPU scheduling involves determining which process in the ready queue should be allocated the CPU at any given time.

- Various CPU scheduling algorithms are used to make this decision, including:
- First come first serve scheduling
- Shortest Job First (SJF) Scheduling
- Priority Scheduling
- Shortest Remaining Time (SRT) Scheduling
- Round Robin (RR) Scheduling
- Multilevel Queue Scheduling
- Multilevel Feedback Queue Scheduling

2.7.1 FCFS – First Come First Serve Scheduling

1. The first process to seek CPU time is run first, according to the First Come First Serve (FCFS) algorithm, which distributes the CPU to the first process that arrives.
2. First In, First Out (FIFO) scheduling is how this system works.
3. It is a non-preemptive scheduling technique, which means that once a process begins, it will not be stopped until it is finished.
4. FCFS is easy to comprehend and apply.
5. But in terms of performance, it is not very effective because the average waiting time is usually long, particularly when shorter operations must wait for larger ones.

Common Terms for Calculation in Process Scheduling:

- **Arrival Time:** The moment when each task enters the CPU scheduling queue is known as the "arrival time."
- **Completion Time:** The amount of time after arrival at which a process completes its execution.
- **Turnaround Time:** The difference between the arrival time and the completion time, which represents the overall amount of time needed to finish a procedure.
- **Waiting Time:** The amount of time a process waits in the ready queue before beginning to execute is known as the waiting time. It is computed as the difference between the process's turnaround time and burst time.

CPU Scheduling Algorithms

- FCFS → First Come First Serve.
- SJF → Shortest Job First.
- SRT → Shortest Remaining Time.
- Priority based scheduling.
- Round robin based scheduling.

FCFS

Process	Arrival time (AT)	Burst time (BT)	Completion time (CT)	Turnaround time (TAT) CT – AT	Waiting time (WT) TAT – BT
P_0	0	5	5	5	0
P_1	1	3	8	7	4
P_2	2	8	16	14	6
P_3	3	6	22	19	13

Gantt chart

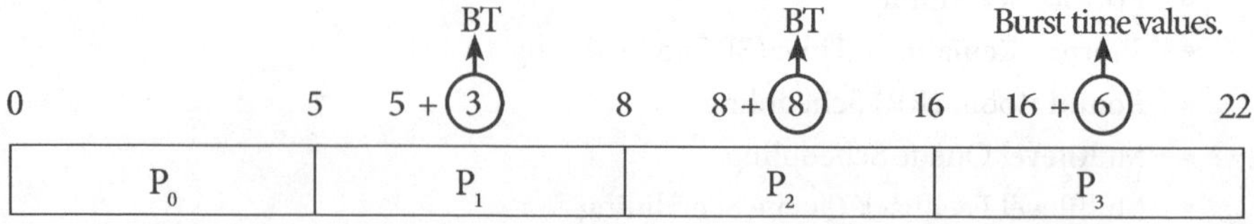

- Completion time values are found by using Gantt chart.

$$\text{Avg. (TAT)} = \frac{\text{tot(TAT)}}{\text{no. of process}} = \frac{5+7+14+19}{4}$$

$$= \frac{45}{4} = \boxed{11.25 \text{ msec.}}$$

$$\text{Avg. (WT)} = \frac{0+4+6+13}{4} = \frac{23}{4} = \boxed{5.75 \text{ msec.}}$$

2.7.2 SJF – Shortest Job First Scheduling

This scheduling algorithm is also referred to as Shortest Job Next (SJN).

- Both preemptive and non-preemptive are possible.
- It is thought to be the most effective strategy for cutting down on waiting times.
- In batch systems, when the amount of CPU time needed for each task is known in advance, it is simple to implement.
- In interactive systems, when it is impossible to estimate ahead of time how much CPU time each operation would use, it is unworkable.
- The system has to know in advance how long each operation will take in order for this algorithm to work correctly.

SJF

(check notes for explanation) →

- Shortest Job First
- Non – Preemptive

AT → Arrival time
BT → Burst time
CT → Completion time
TAT → Turnaround time
WT → Waiting time

Process	AT	BT	CT	TAT	WT
P_0	0	7	7	7	0
P_1	2	4	12	10	6
P_2	4	1	8	4	3
P_3	5	4	16	11	7
				Total = 32	**Total = 16**

Gantt chart

0 | 7 | 7 + 1 | 8 | 8 + 4 | 12 | 12 + 4 | 16

P_0	P_2	P_1	P_3

$$\text{Avg. (TAT)} = \frac{32}{4}$$

$$= \boxed{8 \text{ msec.}}$$

∵ P_0 & P_1 are shortest processes.

∵ P_0 completed.

∵ P_1 P_2 P_3 are remaining in queue

$$\text{Avg. (WT)} = \frac{16}{4}$$

$$= \boxed{4\text{ msec.}}$$

∵ $\xrightarrow{P_1 P_2 P_3}$ ⇒ BT values
4 1 4

∵ In the above processes check BT values.

∵ P_2 is small.

∵ Remaining P_1 P_3 with same BT values.

∵ Take small process as $P_1 \rightarrow$ first
$P_3 \rightarrow$ last

2.7.3 Priority Based Scheduling

Priority scheduling is a non-pre-emptive algorithm and is widely used in batch systems.

The highest priority procedure is carried out first, then the next highest, and so on. Every process is assigned a priority. When many processes have the same priority, they are carried out in order of priority. A process's memory demands, time requirements, and other resource requirements can all affect how important it is.

Priority Based Scheduling

Process	Priority	AT	BT	CT	TAT (CT – AT)	WT (TAT – BT)
P_0	3	0	7	7	7	0
P_1	2	2	4	15	13	9
P_2	4	4	1	16	12	11
P_3	1	5	4	11	6	2

Gantt chart

P_0 & P_3 ⇒ Low & High process.
1 → High } **check with process**
3 → Low } **& priority values.**

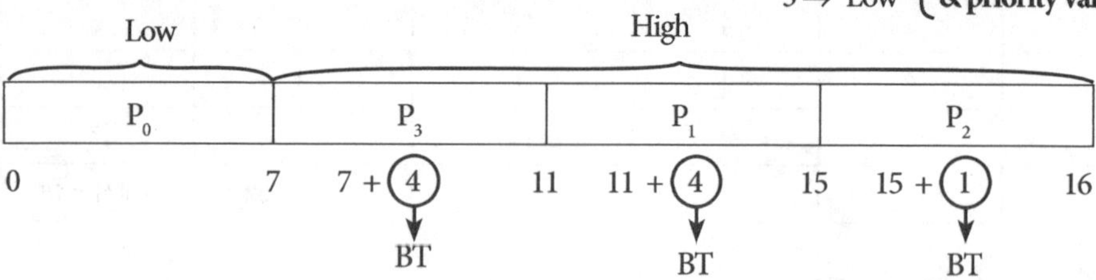

$$\text{Avg (TAT)} = \frac{38}{4}$$

$$= \boxed{9.5\text{ msec.}}$$

$$\text{Avg (WT)} = \frac{22}{4}$$

$$= \boxed{5.5\text{ msec.}}$$

∵ First finish off the P_0 process. Since it is low priority.

∵ Next High priority with P_1 P_2 P_3 processes.

∵ Start with (P_3) with BT value 4 (↑ 1)

P_3: 1 → High

∵ Next P_1 with BT value 4

P_1 : 2 → High

∵ Next P_0 we completed already.$_1$

∵ Next P_2 with BT value 1

P_2 : 4 → High

2.7.4 SRT – Shortest Remaining Time Scheduling

A newer job with an even shorter remaining time may preempt the processor, which is allocated to the work with the shortest remaining time to completion.

- Similar to SJN, it is not feasible in interactive systems when it is unknown how much CPU time each operation would need beforehand. It is frequently employed in batch settings when prioritizing shorter tasks is the main goal.

SRT

- Shortest Remaining Time
- preemptive (A process is pause the process so switching over to another process depending upon some criteria.)

Process	AT	BT	CT	TAT (CT – AT)	WT (TAT – BT)
P_0	0	7	16	16	9
P_1	2	4	7	5	1
P_2	4	1	5	1	0
P_3	5	4	11	6	2

Gantt chart:

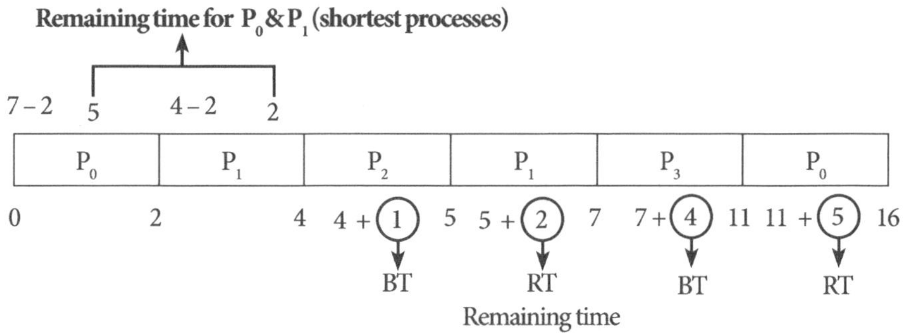

$$\text{Avg (TAT)} = \frac{28}{4} = \boxed{7 \text{ msec.}}$$

∵ P_0 & P_1 are the two shortest processes.

∵ As given in the name we need to find remaining time (RT) for P_0 & P_1

$\Rightarrow P_0 = \text{BT} \rightarrow 7, \; \text{AT} \rightarrow 2 \; \} \; 7 - 2 = $ **5**

$$\text{Avg (WT)} = \frac{12}{4} = \boxed{3 \text{ msec.}}$$

$$\left.\begin{array}{l} P_1 = BT \rightarrow 4 \\ \quad\;\; AT \rightarrow 2 \end{array}\right\} \begin{array}{l} 4-2 \\ 2 \end{array}$$

∵ Other P_2 & P_3 are calculated with BT.

2.7.5 Round Robin Scheduling

Round Robin is a pre-emptive process scheduling algorithm.

- Every process is given a quantum, or set amount of time, to complete. A process is pre-empted once it has completed its allotted time, and the subsequent process is given an opportunity to complete its own time frame. The pre-empted processes' state is saved by context switching, enabling them to continue running when their time comes around.

Round Robin Based Scheduling

Quantum value = 3 msec.

Also called as time slice.

Process	AT	BT	CT	CT – AT TAT	TAT – BT WT
P_0	0	7	21	21	14
P_1	2	4	14	12	8
P_2	4	1	10	6	5

Quantum: Maximum time CPU given to the process at a single point of time.

Short process (P_0, P_1)

P_0	P_1	P_0	P_2	P_1	P_0
0 – 3	3+3 – 6	6+3 – 9	9+1 – 10	10+4 – 14	14+7 – 21

$$\text{Avg. (TAT)} = \frac{39}{4} = \boxed{9.75 \text{ msec.}}$$

$$\text{Avg. (WT)} = \frac{27}{4} = \boxed{6.75 \text{ msec.}}$$

∵ P_0 & P_1 are short process add with the quantum values.

∵ And after that all the three processes are added with tha Burst time (BT) values.

2.8 DIFFERENCES BETWEEN PREEMPTIVE SCHEDULING AND NON-PREEMPTIVE SCHEDULING

Preemptive Scheduling	Non-Preemptive Scheduling
Processor can be preempted to executive a different process in the middle of execution of any current process.	Once Processor starts to execute a process it must finish it before executing the other. It cannot be paused in middle.

Preemptive Scheduling	Non-Preemptive Scheduling
CPU utilization is more compared to Non-Preemptive Scheduling.	CPU utilization is less compared to Preemptive Scheduling.
Waiting time and response time is less.	Waiting time and Response time is more.
The preemptive scheduling is prioritized. The highest priority process should always be the process that is currently utilized.	When a process enters the state of running, the state of that process is not deleted from the scheduler until it finishes its service time.
If a high priority process frequently arrives in the ready queue, low priority process may starve.	If a process with long burst time is running CPU, then another process with less CPU burst time may starve.
Preemptive scheduling is flexible.	Non-preemptive scheduling is rigid.
Ex: SRTF, Priority, Round Robin, etc.	Ex: FCFS, SJF, Priority, etc.

Multiple-Level Queues Scheduling

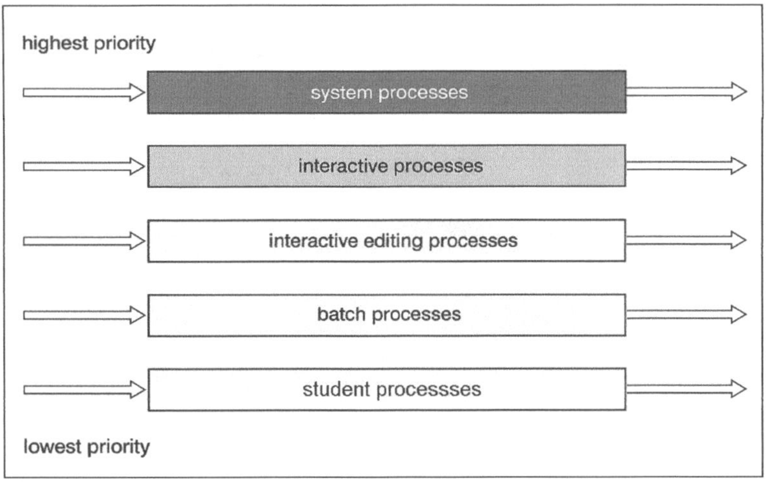

Fig. 2.11: *Multiple Level Queues Scheduling*

Multiple-level queues are not a scheduling algorithm in and of itself; rather, they organize and schedule processes with similar properties by leveraging other existing algorithms.

A number of queues are kept up to date, each with processes that have similar characteristics. Every queue has the ability to employ a unique scheduling method. Each queue is given a priority, which dictates the sequence in which processes are scheduled.

Multilevel Feedback Queue Scheduling

In the multilevel queue scheduling algorithm, processes are typically assigned to a queue permanently when they first enter the system.

On the other hand, processes can switch between queues according to their behavior thanks to the multilayer feedback-queue scheduling method. Sorting processes according to their CPU burst characteristics is the goal. A process gets relegated to a lower-priority queue if it uses up too much CPU time. I/O-bound and interactive processes are guaranteed to stay in higher-priority queues thanks to this mechanism. On the other hand, a process may be shifted to a higher-priority queue if it spends an excessive amount of time in a lower-priority queue. Aging is a strategy that ensures lower-priority processes ultimately get performed, hence preventing hunger.

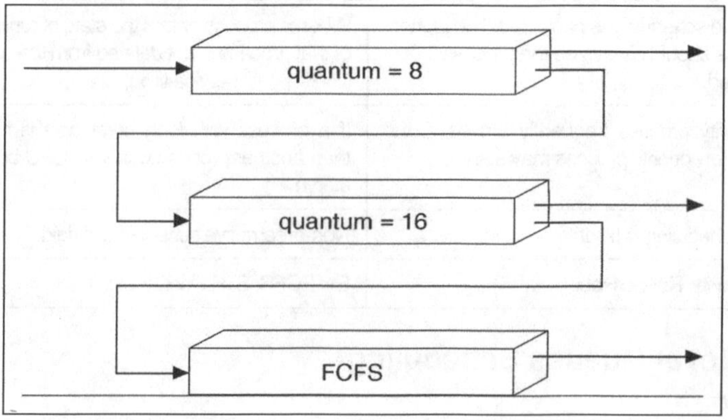

***Fig. 2.12:** Multilevel Feedback Queues*

◆◆◆

UNIT 3

Synchronization and Deadlocks

A cooperative process is one that has the ability to affect or be affected by other processes that are executing in a system. These processes can exchange information via files or messages, or they can access a shared logical address space directly. Lightweight threads or processes are commonly used to implement the first strategy. Concurrent access to shared data, however, may result in irregularities.

It is possible to utilize a bounded buffer to make shared memory access easier. A maximum of BUFFER_SIZE – 1 items can be stored in the buffer in the traditional producer-consumer problem. Adding an integer variable called counter that is initialized to zero is one method to get around this restriction. When an item is removed from the buffer, this counter goes down, and when a new item is added, it goes up. Although the producer and consumer functions operate properly when separated, they can cause unforeseen problems when they are executed simultaneously.

The producer process can be written as follows:

```
while (true) {
/* Generate an item in nextProduced */
while (counter == BUFFER_SIZE); // Wait if the buffer is full buffer[in] = nextProduced;
in = (in + 1) % BUFFER_SIZE;
counter++;
}
```

Similarly, the consumer process can be written as:

```
while (true) {
while (counter == 0); // Wait if the buffer is empty nextConsumed = buffer[out];
out = (out + 1) % BUFFER_SIZE;
counter--;
/* Process the consumed item */
}
```

Both procedures work properly when performed separately, but when they run simultaneously, problems occur.

For example, if the producer and consumer perform the operations counter++ and counter--simultaneously and the counter is now 5, the resultant value of the counter may be 4, 5, or 6 rather than the proper value (5). The way instructions are carried out at the machine level is the cause of this disparity. In assembly-like processes, the statement counter++ can be expressed as follows:

register1 = counter

register1 = register1 + 1

counter = register1

Similarly, counter--executes as:

register2 = counter

register2 = register2 -1

counter = register2

These processes may interleave randomly when they run concurrently, producing inaccurate results.

Examine the execution sequence that follows:

T0: producer execute // register1 = counter {registry = 5}

T1: producer execute // register 1 = register1 + 1 {registry = 6}

T2: consumer execute // register2 = counter {register2 — 5}

T3: consumer execute // register2 = register2 — 1 {register 2 — 4}

T4: producer execute // counter = register1 {counter = 6}

T5: consumer execute // counter = register2 {counter = 4}

Following these actions, the counter is mistakenly set to 4 rather than 5, displaying a typical race condition. When several processes access and alter shared data at the same time and the outcome is dependent on the order of execution, this is known as a race condition. Process synchronization, which makes sure that only one process at a time alters the counter variable, is required to avoid such inconsistencies.

3.1 THE CRITICAL SECTION PROBLEM

Each process in a system has a vital chunk of code that allows it to do actions that require special access, update tables, or modify shared variables. To avoid disputes, only one process should ever complete its essential part.

The critical section challenge involves developing a protocol that allows processes to coordinate their access to common resources. Each operation must obtain authorization before approaching its critical phase. This request is handled by the code's entering section, which is followed by the exit section after the crucial part is complete. The remaining part of the process is referred to as the residual section.

General Structure of a Process (Pi)

```
do {
Entry Section;
Critical Section;
Exit Section;
Remainder Section;
} while (TRUE);
```

A crucial section allows just one thread to run at a time. While the others wait (or "sleep"), only one thread is allowed to enter at a time. The OS schedules the execution of other processes until the essential part becomes available.

Requirements for an Acceptable Solution

A correct solution to the critical section problem must satisfy the following three conditions:

1. **Mutual Exclusion:** When a process is working in a critical region, no other process may access that area at the same time.
2. **Progress:** If no process is in its critical phase and some processes want to enter, the next process's selection cannot be postponed indefinitely.
3. **Bounded Waiting:** There should be a limit on how many times other processes can enter after a process submits an access request before the request is granted.

Two-Process Solutions

Algorithm 1 (Strict Alternation)

```
do {
while (turn != i);
Critical Section;
turn = j;
Remainder Section;
} while (1);
```

This method ensures mutual exclusion, however it fails to meet the progress condition. If turn == 0 and P1 wants to enter the critical part, it cannot proceed even if P0 is in its remaining section.

Algorithm 2 (Flag-Based Solution)

```
do {
flag[i] = true;
while (flag[j]); // Wait if the other process is in its critical section Critical Section;
flag[i] = false;
Remainder Section;
} while (1);
```

Although progress is not assured, this solution guarantees mutual exclusion. Both processes will enter an endless waiting loop and be unable to proceed if they set their flags at the same time.

P0 and P1 cannot ever be in the critical section simultaneously due to mutual exclusion: If P0 is in its critical section, then flag [0] is true and either turn is 0 (indicating that P1 is just now attempting to enter the crucial area, but is politely waiting) or flag [1] is false (indicating that P1 has left its critical part). When P0 is in the crucial section, P1 cannot be in the critical section in either scenario. Step 6: Progress If another process has set its flag to indicate that it wants to enter its critical section, the first process cannot get back into the crucial section right away.

Boundary waiting: A method that doesn't wait more than one turn to enter the critical area is known as boundary waiting. After giving the other process priority, this process will finish and set its flag to 0, enabling the other process to proceed to the critical phase.

Algorithm 3

By combining the key ideas of algorithm 1 and 2, we obtain a correct solution.

```
do{
Flag[i] =true; Turn = j;
While(flag[j] && turn==j); Critical section
Flag[i] = false; Remainder section
} while(1);
```

The method satisfies the three requirements needed to solve the critical section problem. Progress, restricted waiting, and mutual exclusion are the three prerequisites.

Synchronization Hardware

Any solution to the critical section problem requires the use of a simple instrument called a lock. Race circumstances are prevented by requiring that key areas be locked, meaning that a process must acquire a lock before entering a vital portion and release the lock after exiting the critical section.

```
do {
Acquire Lock
Critical Section Release Lock Remainder Section
} while(TRUE);
```

Solution to the Critical-Section Problem Using Locks

Hardware features can make every programming task easier and boost system efficiency. The critical section problem in a single processor context might be readily fixed if we could prevent interrupts while a shared variable was being modified. Next, we may ensure that the current sequence of instructions can continue uninterrupted.

The shared variable could not be changed unexpectedly because no further commands would be run. This solution is not feasible in a multiprocessor environment. Turning off interruptions on a multiprocessor system can be a lengthy operation because the message is sent to each processor.

```
boolean TestAndSet(boolean *target)
{
boolean rv=target;
*target = TRUE; return rv;
}
```

The definition of the TestAndSet() instruction. do

```
{
while(TestAndSetLock(&lock))
; // do nothing
// critical section lock = FALSE;
//remainder section
}while(TRUE);
```

Mutual-Exclusion Implementation with TestAndSet()

Hardware features can make every programming task easier and boost system efficiency. The critical section problem in a single processor context might be readily fixed if we could prevent interrupts while a shared variable was being modified. Next, we may ensure that the current sequence of instructions can continue uninterrupted. The shared variable could not be changed unexpectedly because no further commands would be run. This solution is not feasible in a multiprocessor environment. Turning off interruptions on a multiprocessor system can be a lengthy operation because the message is sent to each processor.

Two words' contents are affected by the Swap() instruction:

```
Void swap(boolean *a, boolean *b)
{
boolean temp = *a;
*a = *b;
*b = temp;
}
```

Definition of Swap Instruction do

```
{
key=TRUE; while(key==TRUE) swap(&lock, &key);
// critical section lock = FALSE;
// remainder section
}while(TRUE);
```

Mutual Exclusion Implementation with the Swap() function

This is also done in an atomic manner. If the processor implements the Swap() instruction, a global Boolean variable lock initialized to false can be used to accomplish mutual exclusion.

Each process has a local Boolean variable key.

Nevertheless, the bounded-waiting criterion is not satisfied by these approaches. The following algorithm fixes all of the important section problems: The following data structures are commonly used by this algorithm:

Boolean lock; Boolean waiting[n];

These two data structures have false as their initial values. To show that the mutual exclusion requirement is met, we must make sure that process Pi can only reach its essential portion if either waiting[i] == false or key == false. The key's value can only turn false when TestAndSet() is executed.

3.2 SEMAPHORE

In operating systems, a semaphore is a synchronization tool used to control access to shared resources by multiple processes, preventing conflicts and ensuring orderly access, often implemented as a counter that processes can wait on or signal.

In the wait() and signal() actions, modifications to the semaphore's integer value must be executed independently. One process has the ability to change the same semaphore value simultaneously with no other processes.

```
Wait:                     Signal:
Wait(S)                   signal(S)
{                         {
While S<=0;               S++; S--;
}                         }
```

```
do{ waiting(mutex);
//critical section Signal(mutex);
//remainder section
}while(true);
```

Operating systems distinguish between counting semaphores and binary semaphores. The value of a counting semaphore can span an infinite domain. Only values between 0 and 1 can be stored in a binary semaphore. Binary semaphores are also known as mutex locks since they provide mutual exclusion. Binary semaphores solve the critical section problem for many processes. Counting semaphores can be used to control access to a resource with a limited number of instances. The semaphore is initialized using the quantity of available resources. The semaphore and the wait() method are used by each process that wishes to use a resource.

When a process releases a resource, it performs a signal() operation. Semaphores can be used to tackle a variety of synchronization problems. A simple illustration of a binary semaphore with two operations. Two processes are competing for the single semaphore. Since Process A finishes the acquisition first, it is granted the semaphore. The period of time that the process possesses the semaphore is a vital section. The semaphore must be synchronized since only one process may finish the crucial phase. Even when Process A has the semaphore, Process B cannot perform its important function.

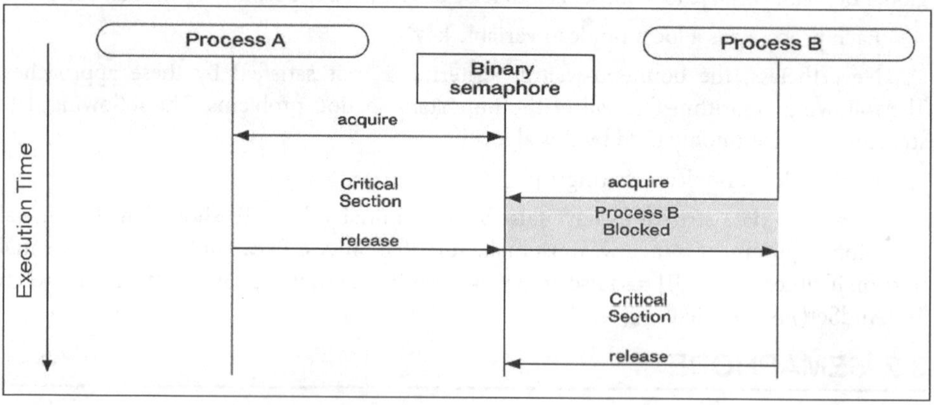

Fig. 3.1: Binary Semaphore

Remember that when Process A is in its critical section, Process B attempts to acquire the semaphore. Since Process A has already acquired the semaphore, Process B is placed in a blocked state. When Process A finally releases the semaphore, enabling it to proceed to its critical phase, Process B receives it. Process B subsequently releases the semaphore, enabling acquisition.

Two resources are required for each process in the counting semaphore example to complete its designated responsibilities. Only one process will be permitted to operate at full capacity simultaneously because the counting semaphore in this example has a value of 3. Since Process A acquires its two resources first, Process B waits for Process A to relinquish at least one of its resources.

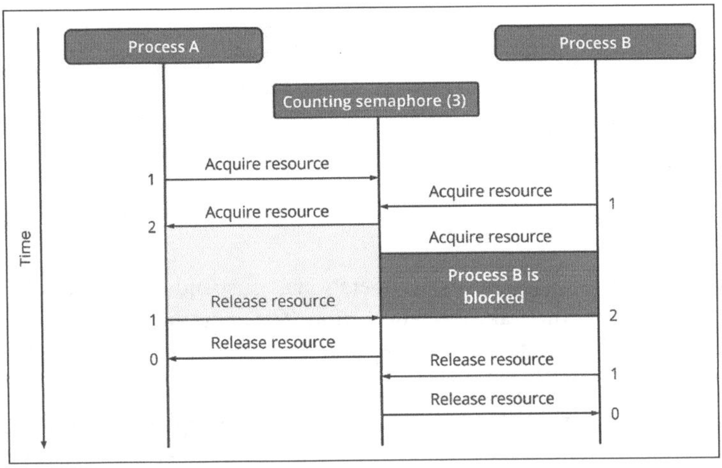

Fig. 3.2: Counting Semaphore

Execution

The requirement for busy waiting is the main disadvantage of the semaphore. While a process is in its crucial part, any other process that tries to enter that region must continuously loop in the entry code. Busy waiting wastes CPU cycles that could be better utilized by another task. This type of semaphore is called a spinlock because the process revolves while it awaits the lock. The necessity for busy waiting can be circumvented by altering the definition of the wait() and signal() semaphore operations.

When a process uses the wait() method and finds that the semaphore value is not positive, it has to wait. Rather than using busy waiting, the process might block itself. When another process performs a signal() operation, a stalled process that is waiting on a semaphore S should be restarted. A wakeup() operation is used to resume the process, transforming it from the waiting state to the ready state. After that, the process is added to the ready queue.

To implement semaphores under this definition, we define a semaphore as a "C" struct:

```
typedef struct { int
value;
struct process *list;
} semaphore;
```

Each semaphore contains an integer value and a list of processes. When a process must wait on a semaphore, it is added to the list of processes. A signal() operation wakes up one process and removes it from the list of waiting processes. A signal() operation wakes up one process and removes it from the list of waiting processes.

Wait() semaphore operation can be defined as

```
wait(semaphore *S) { S->value—;
if (S->value < 0) {
add this process to S->list; block();
}
}
```

Signal() semaphore operation can be defined as signal(semaphore *S) {

```
S->value++;
if (S->value <= 0) {
remove a process P from S->list; wakeup(P);
}
}
```

The process that initiates the block operation is suspended. A blocked process P's execution is resumed via the wakeup(P) operation. The operating system offers these two functions as fundamental system calls. Keep in mind that while semaphores are defined according to the traditional concept

Although this implementation may have negative semaphore values, busy waiting ensures that the semaphore value is always positive. The number of processes waiting on the semaphore is its magnitude if the semaphore value is negative. This fact arises from the implementation of the wait() action in which the order of the test and the decrement is switched.

The list of pending processes can be easily implemented thanks to the link field found in each process control block (PCB). Each semaphore contains an integer value and a pointer to a list of PCBs. One way to add and remove processes from the list while preserving constrained waiting is to use a FIFO queue, where the semaphore holds both head and tail pointers to the queue. Nonetheless, the list can often use any queueing method. Proper semaphor usage does not require a particular queueing strategy for the semaphore lists. The atomic execution of semaphores is their key characteristic. For wait() and signal() operations, we must ensure that no two processes can utilize the same semaphore at the same time.

By simply blocking interrupts while the wait() and signal() methods are in use, we can get around this critical-section issue in a single-processor scenario, where there is only one CPU. This method works in a single processor environment since once interrupts are muted, instructions from different processes cannot be interleaved. Only the active process keeps running until interruptions are enabled once more and the scheduler takes back control.

In order to avoid uncontrolled interleaving of instructions from several processes (running on different processors), interrupts must be disabled on each processor in a multiprocessor system. Disabling interrupts on every CPU may be difficult, but it can drastically lower performance.

Therefore, SMP systems must include alternative locking mechanisms, like as spinlocks, to ensure that wait() and signal() are executed atomically. It must be acknowledged that busy waiting has not completely disappeared with this specification of the wait() and signal() functions. Rather, we have removed busy waiting from the critical regions of the application programs' entry portion.

3.3 CLASSIC PROBLEMS OF SYNCHRONIZATION

Examples of the broad category of concurrency control issues include these synchronization issues. Semaphores are used to synchronize solutions to these issues.

3.3.1 The Bounded Buffer Problem

In this case, the pool is made up of n buffers, each of which may retain one item. The mutex semaphore is initialized to the value 1 and offers mutual exclusion for buffer pool access. The number of empty and full buffers is counted by the empty and full semaphores. The initial values of the semaphore full and empty are set to 0 and n, respectively.

The following code can be seen as either the consumer creating empty buffers for the producer or the producer creating filled buffers for the consumer.

The structure of the **Producer Process** is as follows:

```
do
{
// produce an item in nextp wait(empty); wait(mutex);
// add the item to the buffer signal(mutex);
signal(full);
}while(TRUE);
```

The structure of the **Consumer Process** is as follows:

```
do
{
wait(full); wait(mutex);
// remove an item from buffer into nextc signal(mutex); signal(empty);
// consume the item in nextc
}while(TRUE);
```

3.3.2 The Readers – Writers Problem

A database is intended to be shared by several running programs. Some of these programs (readers) may just want to read the database, while others (writers) may want to update it. If two readers examine the shared data simultaneously, there won't be any detrimental effects.

When a writer and another thread access the database simultaneously, problems occur. To circumvent these problems, only writers have access to the shared database. This synchronization difficulty is known as the readers-writers dilemma.

```
do { wait(wrt);
//Writing is Performed signal(wrt);
}while(True);
```

The Structure of a Writer Process

The simplest readers According to the writer's issue, no reader should be kept waiting until the writer has already obtained permission to access the shared object. Readers shouldn't wait for other readers to finish just because a writer is waiting.

```
do {
wait(mutex);
readcount++;
if(readcount==1)
wait(wrt);
signal(mutex);
// reading is performed
wait(mutex);
readcount--;
if(readcount==0)
signal(wrt);
signal(mutex);
} while(True);
```

3.3.3 The Structure of a Reader Process

The secondary readers The challenge for writers is to write as quickly as possible after they are ready; if they wait to access the object, no new readers will begin writing. The reader processes in the first readers-writers problem solution share the following data structures:

The semaphore

mutex, wrt;

int readcount;

Readcount is set to 0 and the semaphores mutex and wrt are set to 1. Both writer and reader processes use semaphore wrt. When the variable readcount is updated, mutual exclusion is ensured by the mutex semaphore. The number of processes reading the object at any given time is monitored by the readcount variable. For the authors, the semaphore serves as a mutual exclusion semaphore. The reader who enters or quits the critical area first or last also uses it. Readers who come in or go out while other readers are in their crucial part do not use it.

In order to give reader-writer locks on certain systems, the readers-writer problem and its solutions have been generalized. Selecting the lock's mode—read or write access—is necessary to obtain the reader-writer lock. If a process wants to read shared data, it asks for the reader-writer lock in read mode; if it wants to change shared data, it needs to ask for the lock in write mode. While many processes can simultaneously obtain a reader-writer lock in read mode, only one process can obtain the lock for writing since writers need exclusive access.

Reader – writer locks are useful in the following situations:

In applications where it is simple to determine which threads only write shared data and which processes only read it. In applications where the number of readers exceeds the number of writers.

3.3.4 Dining Philosophers Problem

Identify five thinkers who spend their days eating and reflecting. The philosophers share a circular table and are seated around it in five chairs, each of which belongs to a different philosopher. A bowl of rice is set in the center of the table, along with five single chopsticks. While pondering, a philosopher does not interact with her contemporaries. Sometimes a philosopher gets hungry and tries to grab the two chopsticks closest to her. A philosopher can only hold one chopstick at a time. She can't pick up the neighbor's chopstick when she's holding it.

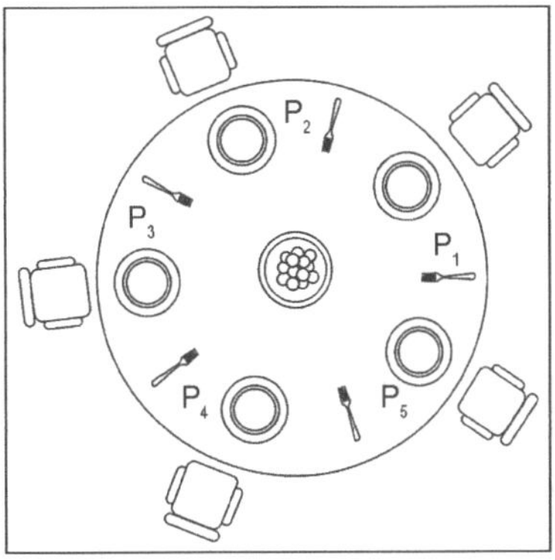

Fig. 3.3: Dining Philosopher

When a hungry philosopher eats with both chopsticks in her hand, she does not take them away. After eating, she puts down both chopsticks and goes back to thinking. The supper philosopher's dilemma is considered a classic synchronization problem and serves as an example of a large class of concurrency control problems. A simple solution to this issue is to use a semaphore to represent each chop stick.

A philosopher tries to seize a chop stick by conducting a wait () action on that semaphore, then releases it by performing the signal () operation on the relevant semaphores. Therefore, the shared data is semaphore chopsticks [5], where all chopstick components are initialized to 1.

This method is not recommended since it may lead to a deadlock. Assume that when the five philosophers all become hungry at the same moment, they each reach for their left chopstick. By now, all of the chopstick's parts will be equal to zero. She will reach for her right chopstick, causing each philosopher to be eternally delayed.

The structure of **dinning philosopher problem** is as follows:

```
do
{
wait(chopstick[i]); wait(chopstick[(i+ 1)
% 5] );
//eat signal(chopstick[i]); signal(chopstick[(i+ 1) % 5] );
//think
}while(TRUE);
```

The solution to the dining philosopher's dilemma is to:

- Limit the number of philosophers who can sit at a table at once to four; only allow a philosopher to take up her chopsticks if both are available. Use an asymmetrical strategy in which an odd philosopher picks up her left chopstick first, then her right, while an even philosopher picks up her right chopstick first, then her left.

3.4 CRITICAL REGIONS

A portion of code that is always run under mutual exclusion is known as a critical zone. When semaphores are utilized, critical zones transfer the burden of enforcing mutual exclusion from the programmer to the compiler. They are divided into two sections:

1. Variables subject to mutual exclusion that need to be accessed.
2. A new language declaration that pinpoints a crucial area where the variables are retrieved

```
var v : shared T;
...
region v do
begin
...
end;
```

All critical regions that are 'tagged' with the same variable have compiler-enforced mutual exclusion so that only one of them can be executed at a time:

```
Process A:
region V1 do begin
{ Do some stuff. } end; region V2 do
begin
{ Do more stuff. } end;
Process B:
region V1 do begin
{ Do other stuff. } end;
```

If both processes want to function within their respective V1 territories, then only one of them may continue, even though process A may be working within its V2 region and process Bis is operating within its V1 territory. Each of the shared variables (V1 and V2 above) has a queue associated with it.

Once a process has started executing code inside a region designated with the same variable, any subsequent attempts by other processes to access that zone are prevented and added to the queue.

Conditional Critical Regions

Critical zones are not the same as semaphores. Their conditions are not synchronized. Although critical regions prevent this from occurring, semaphores can be used to stop a process until a specific condition is met (see, for instance, the bounded-buffer Producer-Consumer problem). Conditional critical regions are used to achieve condition synchronization for critical regions:

```
region v when B do
begin
...
end;
```

where B is a boolean expression (usually B will refer to v).

Conditional important regions operate as follows:

1. To enter a zone for v, a process needs to gain the mutex lock. If it cannot, it is queued.
2. After acquiring the lock, the boolean expression B is examined. If B evaluates to true, the process proceeds; if not, the lock and queues are released. When it gets the lock again, it must retest B.

Implementation

Each shared variable now has two queues associated with it. The main queue contains processes that want to access a critical area but find it locked. The event queue contains the processes that stopped because they thought the condition was false. When a process leaves the conditional critical region, the processes in the event queue merge with those in the main queue. Because they must retest their condition, these processes are participating in something akin to busy-waiting, even though they will retest the state far less frequently. Furthermore, note that the condition is only retested because there is reason to believe that it may have changed (for example, because another process has finished accessing the shared variable). Though this is more controlled than busy-waiting, it may nevertheless be sufficiently near to it to be unappealing.

Limitations

- The protected variables cannot be changed;
- No information is hidden or encapsulated;
- Conditional important parts are still scattered throughout the program code.
- Once inside a crucial zone, a process can do anything it wants to the variables to which it has exclusive access.
- Compared to semaphores, conditional critical zones are more difficult to implement successfully.

3.5 MONITORS

Because semaphores only happen when certain execution sequences are followed, which isn't always the case, improper use of them can result in timing errors that are difficult to detect even if they provide a useful and effective mechanism to synchronize processes. Imagine that a process alternates between performing the signal() and wait() procedures on the semaphore mutex in a different order.

Signal (mutex);

....

Critical section

....

Wait (mutex);

In this case, the mutual exclusion condition may be broken by multiple processes operating concurrently in their key portions. * Assume that a process executes when it substitutes the wait mutex for the signal mutex.

Wait(mutex);

......

Critical section

.... Wait(mutex);

There will be a deadlock here.

Assume that a procedure either leaves out the signal (mutex), the wait (mutex), or both. In this case, a dead lock will happen or mutual exclusion will be broken. A basic high level synchronization component known as monitor type is used to address such issues.

Use

Programmer-defined operations that are mutually exclusive within the monitor are displayed by a monitor type. The declaration of variables whose values indicate the state of an instance of that type is part of the monitor type, as are the bodies of the functions or procedures that deal with those variables. The representation of a monitor type cannot be used directly by the various processes. Consequently, a method defined within a monitor can access only variables declared locally within the monitor and its formal parameters. The local variables of a monitor are only accessible by the local procedures.

Name:monitor

.....local declarations

.....initialize local data Proc1(....parameters)

......statement list Proc2(...parameters)

.......statement list Proc3(...parameters)

.......statement list

The monitor architecture allows just one process to be active within the monitor at a time. This monitor design, however, is unable to accurately mimic certain synchronization systems. For this, we need more synchronization strategies. These mechanisms are provided by the condition construct. You can only use the signal() and wait() procedures on a condition variable. Until another process calls x.signal(), the action x.wait() suspends the running process. The x.signal() operation resumes exactly one suspended process. When a process P calls the x.signal() operation, a suspended process Q is associated with condition x. If suspended process Q is allowed to continue operating, the signaling process P has to wait. If not, P and Q would be simultaneously active on the monitor.

However, both processes are theoretically capable of being implemented. Two choices are available:

Give a signal, then wait: In this case, P either waits for another condition to happen or for Q to leave the display. In this case, Q waits for another circumstance or for P to get off the display.

Dining Philosophers Solution using Monitors

This solution states that a philosopher can only pick up her chopsticks if both are available. To code this response, we need to distinguish between the three states where a philosopher could be located. For this, we make use of this data structure. A philosopher Only when her two neighbors are not eating can I set the variable state[i] = eating. enum {thinking, hungry, eating} state[5]; the states [(i+4)%5]! and [(i+1)%5]! stand for eating. Additionally, declare condition self [5] so that the philosopher might delay when she is hungry but unable to obtain the chopsticks she desires. The distribution of

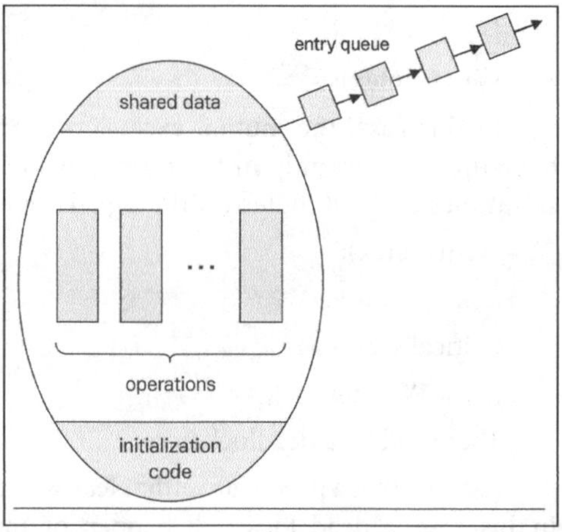

Fig. 3.4.

the chopsticks is controlled by the monitor dp. Each philosopher must utilize the pickup() function before starting to eat.

The philosopher process might be suspended as a result of this. The philosopher can eat once the procedure is successfully finished. The putdown() procedure is then called by the philosopher. Philosopher I must therefore call pickup() and putdown() in the order listed below:

dp.pickup(i);

……. Eat

……. dp.putdown(i);

This solution ensures that no two neighbors are eating simultaneously and that no deadlocks will occur

Implementing a Monitor using Semaphores

For each monitor, a semaphore mutex initialized to 1 is provided. A process must execute wait (mutex) before entering the monitor and execute (signal) after leaving the monitor. Since a signaling process needs to wait until the resumed process either leaves or waits, an additional semaphore is then initialized to 0 on which the signaling processes may suspend themselves. An integer variable named next_count is used to count the number of processes suspended on next. As a result, each external procedure P is replaced by wait(mutex);

body of F

if (next_count > 0) signal(next); else

signal(mutex);

Mutual exclusion within a monitor is thus ensured.

We can now describe how condition variables are implemented. For each condition x, we introduce a semaphore x_sem and an integer variable

x_count, both initialized to 0. The operation x. wait () can now be implemented as x_count++; if (next_count > 0)

signal(next);

else signal(mutex); wait(x_sem); x_count—;

The operation x. signal () can be implemented as if (x_count > 0) {

next_count++; signal(x_sem); wait(next) ; next_count—; }

Resuming Processes Within a Monitor

When x.signal() is run, the process with the lowest related priority number is restarted. We employ FCFS ordering to decide which suspended process should be resumed next if several processes are suspended on condition x and one of those processes performs an x.signal() operation. An alternative use case for conditional wait construct() is x.wait(c); in which c is an integer expression evaluated upon execution of the wait () operation, and the value of c, which is also referred to as a priority number, is saved with the name of the suspended process.

monitor ResourceAllocator boolean busy;

condition x;

void acquire(int time) if (busy) x.wait(time);

busy = TRUE; void release() { busy = FALSE; x.signal();

initialization_code busy = FALSE;

A Monitor to Allocate a Single Resource

We look at the Resource Allocator monitor, which manages how one resource is distributed among conflicting programs. Each process specifies the maximum amount of time it intends to use the resource when seeking its allocation. The process with the smallest timeallocation request receives the resource allocation from the monitor.

A process that needs to access the resource in question must do so in the following order:

Reacquire(t);

access the resource;

R. release () ;

Where R is an instance of type ResourceAllocator. Unfortunately, the monitor concept cannot guarantee that the preceding access sequence will be observed. In particular, the following problems can occur:

- It is possible for a process to access a resource without first obtaining authorization to do so.
- Once a process has been given access to a resource, it may never release it. An example of synchronization is when a process tries to relinquish a resource that it has never requested.
- It is possible for a process to make two requests for the same resource without first releasing it.

Incorporating resource access activities into the ResourceAllocator monitor is one possible way to address the current problem; however, doing so will cause scheduling to follow the built-in monitor-scheduling method instead of the one we have programmed. Our initial motivation for creating the monitor constructions was comparable to the difficulties we encountered when utilizing semaphores. In the past, we had to be concerned about using semaphores correctly. The compiler can no longer assist us with higher-level programmer-defined operations, therefore we now have to worry about using them correctly.

To ensure that the processes follow the correct steps, we must inspect each program that makes use of the ResourceAllocator monitor and its managed resource. We must confirm two needs in order to ascertain whether this system is accurate.

- First and foremost, the monitor must always be called by user processes in the correct sequence.
- Second, by ignoring the mutual-exclusion gateway provided by the monitor, we must ensure that an unfriendly process does not attempt to directly access the shared resource, evading the access protocols.

If these two conditions are satisfied, we can only guarantee that there won't be any time-dependent errors or that the scheduling method won't be beaten.

Although this inspection would be possible for a small, static system, it is not realistic for a big or dynamic system. This access-control problem can only be solved in other ways.

A collection of blocked processes, each of which is holding a resource and is awaiting the acquisition of a resource that another process in the collection is holding. For instance, the system has two tape drives. Semaphores A and B, initialized to 1, are required for each tape drive that P0 and P1 each possess.

P_0

wait (A);

wait (B);

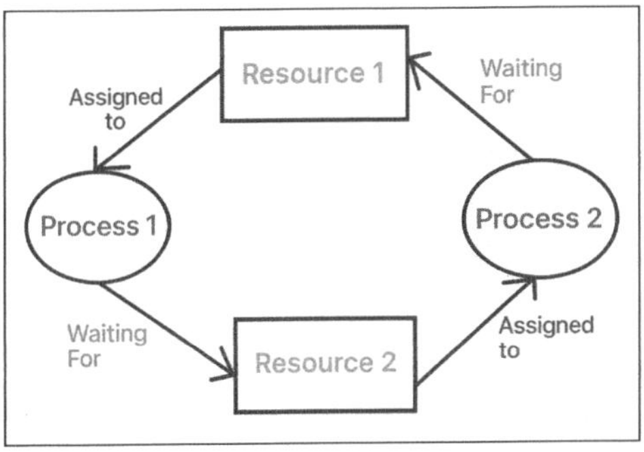

P_1

wait(B);

wait(A);

Fig. 3.5.

Starvation

Starvation: High-priority processes constantly consume resources, making it impossible for low-priority processes to obtain them.

- Starvation occurs when a process requests a resource and the other processes have been using it continually, causing the requesting process to become starved.
- When a process is in starvation, it waits for the CPU to distribute the resource. However, because the other processes are constantly blocking the requested resources, the process must wait endlessly.

3.6 DEADLOCK CHARACTERIZATION

Deadlock may occur if all four requirements are satisfied simultaneously. A resource can only be utilized by one process at a time due to mutual exclusion. When a process with at least one resource is waiting to acquire more resources that are being held by other processes, this is referred to as **"hold and wait."**

No preemption: only the process in possession of a resource may freely release it when that process has completed its task. P0 is waiting for a resource held by P1, P1 is waiting for a resource held by P2, …, Pn–1 is waiting for a resource held by Pn, and P0 is waiting for a resource held by P0. This is known as the **cyclical wait**.

Resource-Allocation Graph

A set of vertices V and a set of edges E.

V is partitioned into two types:

P = {P1, P2, …, Pn}, the set consisting of all the processes in the system.

R = {R1, R2, …, Rm}, the set consisting of all resource types in the system.

Request edge – directed edge P1 → Rj

Assignment edge – directed edge Rj → Pi

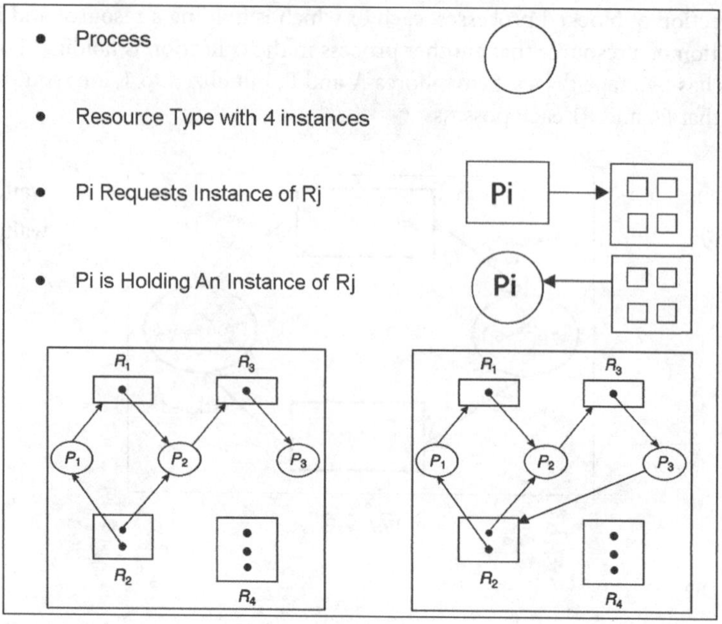

Fig. 3.6.

Facts On Deadlock

- If graph contains no cycles ⇒ no deadlock.
- If graph contains a cycle if only one instance per resource type, then deadlock. if several instances per resource type, possibility of deadlock.

Methods for Handling Deadlocks

- **Preventing or avoiding deadlocks:** Make sure the system never becomes stuck.
- **Deadlock Detection:** Permit a deadlock to occur and then allow the system to recover. Most operating systems, including UNIX, use deadlocks; ignore the issue and act as though they never happen.

3.6.1 Deadlock Prevention

For sharable resources, mutual exclusion is not necessary; for nonsharable resources, it is.

- **Hold and Wait:** This feature ensures that no other resources are held when a process demands a resource. Before a process starts running, it should be required to request and get all of its resources; alternatively, it should be permitted to request resources only when it is in need of them. Low use of resources; potential for famine.
- **No Preemption:** All resources that are presently being held are released if a process that is holding some resources asks for another resource that cannot be assigned to it right away. The list of resources that the process is waiting for is updated with preempted resources. Only when the process is able to recover its previous resources and the new ones it has requested will it be restarted.

- **Circular Wait:** This requires that all resource types be ordered in total and that resource requests be made by each process in ascending order of enumeration.

3.6.2 Deadlock Avoidance

Necessitates the availability of some extra a priori data in the system. The simplest and most practical approach calls for each process to specify the most resources of each kind it might require. To guarantee that there can never be a circular-wait situation, the deadlock-avoidance method dynamically checks the resource allocation state. The maximal demands of the processes and the quantity of resources available and allotted define the resource-allocation state.

3.6.3 Deadlock Detection

- Permit the system to reach a deadlock.
- Algorithm for detection
- Recovery plan

Basic Facts

- Deadlocks are absent when a system is in a safe state.
- Deadlock is possible if a system is in an unsafe state.
- Avoidance ⇒ guarantee that a system won't ever become dangerous.

Safe, Unsafe, Deadlock State

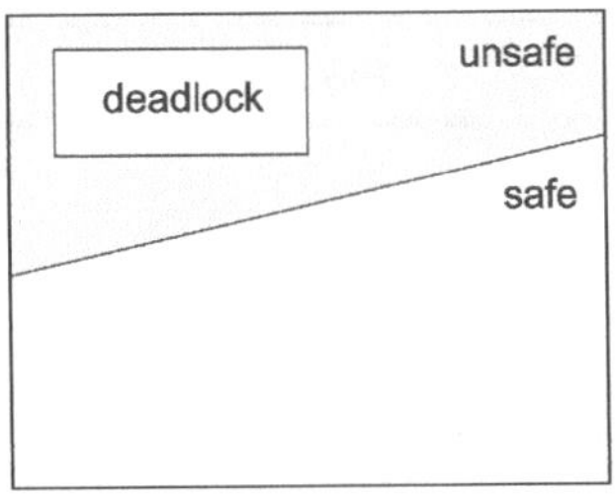

Fig. 3.7.

3.7 RESOURCE-ALLOCATION GRAPH ALGORITHM

Edge of claim Pi → Rj, shown by a dashed line, suggested that process Pj might ask for resource Rj.

- When a process makes a resource request, the claim edge changes to the request edge.
- The assignment edge changes back to a claim edge when a process releases a resource.
- The system requires that resources be claimed beforehand.

Resource-Allocation Graph For Deadlock Avoidance

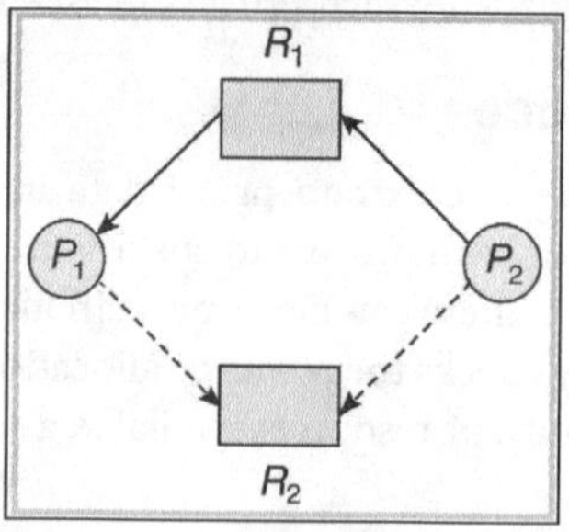

Fig. 3.8.

RAG for Deadlock Avoidance

Unsafe State In Resource-Allocation Graph

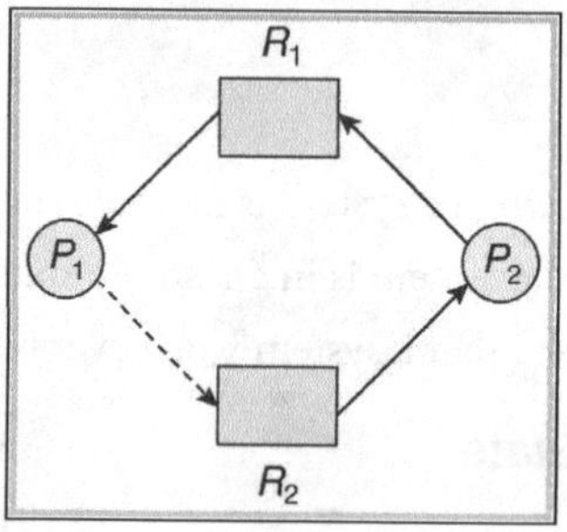

Fig. 3.9.

Unsafe state in RAG

Example:

- Banker's Algorithm
- Resource-Request Algorithm

3.7.1 Banker's Algorithm

Several times.

- Every procedure must assert its utmost use from the outset.
- A process may have to wait when requesting a resource.
- A process has a limited amount of time to return all of its resources.

Data Structures for the Banker's Algorithm

Let m be the number of resource categories and n be the number of processes. A vector of length m is available. There are k instances of resource type Rj available if available

[j] = k. Maximum: matrix of n x m. Process Pi may request a maximum of k instances of resource type Rj if Max [i,j] = k. Allocation: matrix of size n x m. Pi is now assigned k instances of Rj if Allocation[i,j] = k. A n x m matrix is required. Pi might require k additional instances of Rj to finish its task if Need[i,j] = k.

Need [i,j] = Max[i,j] – Allocation [i,j]

Example of Banker's Algorithm

5 processes P0 through P4; 3 resource types A (10 instances), B (5instances), and C (7 instances). Snapshot at time T0:

	Allocation			Max			Available		
	A	B	C	A	B	C	A	B	C
P_0	0	1	0	7	5	3	3	3	2
P_1	2	0	0	3	2	2			
P_2	3	0	2	9	0	2			
P_3	2	1	1	2	2	2			
P_4	0	0	2	4	3	3			

The content of the matrix. Need is defined to be Max – Allocation

	Need		
	A	B	C
P_0	7	4	3
P_1	1	2	2
P_2	6	0	0
P_3	0	1	1
P_4	4	3	1

The system is in a safe state since the sequence < P1, P3, P4, P2, P0> satisfies safety criteria.

Example P1 Request (1,0,2) (Cont.)

	Allocation			Need			Available		
	A	B	C	A	B	C	A	B	C
P_0	0	1	0	7	4	3	2	3	0
P_1	3	0	2	0	2	0			
P_2	3	0	1	6	0	0			
P_3	2	1	1	0	1	1			
P_4	0	0	2	4	3	1			

3.7.2 Detection Algorithm

1. Assume that Work and Finish are vectors with lengths m and n. Set up: a, Work = Available b, For i = 1,2,…,n, Finish[i] = false if Allocationi ≠ 0; else, Finish[i] = true.
2. Determine which index i makes both: a, Finish[i] == false b, Requesti ≤ Work
3. Proceed to step 4 if there isn't a such i. 3. Work + Allocation = Work Start[i] = true to proceed to step 2.
4. The system is in a deadlock condition if Finish[i] == false for some i, 1 < i ≤ n. Furthermore, Pi is stuck if Finish[i] == false.

To determine whether the system is in a deadlocked state, the algorithm needs to do an order of O(m x n2) operations.

Example of Detection Algorithm

Five processes P0 through P4; three resource types A (7 instances), B (2 instances), and C (6 instances). SnapShot at Time T0

	Allocation	Request	Available
	A B C	A B C	A B C
P_0	0 1 0	0 0 0	0 0 0
P_1	2 0 0	2 0 2	
P_2	3 0 3	0 0 0	
P_3	2 1 1	1 0 0	
P_4	0 0 2	0 0 2	

Sequence will result in Finish[i] = true for all i.

	Request
	A B C
P_0	0 0 0
P_1	2 0 1
P_2	0 0 1
P_3	1 0 0
P_4	0 0 2

P2 requests an additional instance of type C.

Can reclaim resources held by process P0, but insufficient resources to fulfill other processes; requests. Deadlock exists, consisting of processes P1, P2, P3, and P4.

Detection-Algorithm Usage

The following determines when and how frequently to invoke:

How frequently is a deadlock likely to happen? What number of procedures will have to be reversed? For every disjoint cycle, one The resource graph may contain numerous cycles if the detection algorithm is called arbitrarily, making it impossible to identify which of the numerous stalled processes "caused" the deadlock.

Recovery from Deadlock: Process Termination

- End all processes that are stuck. Stop one process at a time until the cycle of stalemate is broken.
- What is the best order for us to abort?
- The process's priority.
- How long the process took to calculate and how long it will take to finish?
- The resources utilized by the procedure. The resources process must be finished. The number of processes that must be stopped. Is the process batch or interactive?

Recovery from Deadlock: Resource Preemption:

- Choosing a victim: cut costs.
- Rollback: go back to a secure state and restart the procedure for that state.
- Starvation: The same process can always be chosen as the victim, and the cost factor includes a number of rollbacks.

UNIT 4

Memory Management and I/O Management

4.1 STORAGE / MEMORY MANAGEMENT

Memory management refers to an operating system's capacity to manage or regulate primary memory. Memory management keeps track of all memory locations, whether they are allocated to a task or are free.

It establishes the appropriate amount of memory for every process. It chooses which process receives memory at what time.

It updates the status in accordance with the release or unallocation of memory.

- Memory management uses two registers to offer protection: a base register and a limit register.
- While the base register holds the lowest allowed physical memory address, the limit register shows the size of the range.

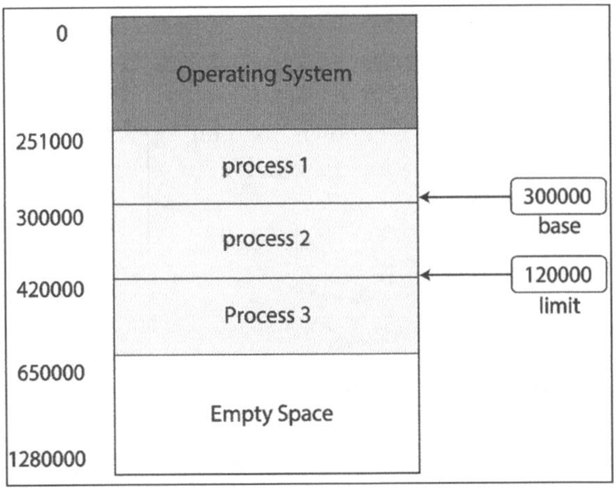

Fig. 4.1.

Goals Of Memory Management

Efficiently distribute available memory among several processes:

- primary functions.
- assign memory to processes as required.
- monitor memory usage and free space.
- shield memory from other processes.

4.2 MEMORY ALLOCATION STRATEGIES

Contiguous Allocation

- In contiguous memory allocation, a single, continuous memory block houses each process.
- Memory is divided into several fixed-size segments.
- Each partition has a single process.
- When a process becomes available, it is selected from the input queue and loaded into a partition.
- The free blocks of memory are called holes.
- The group of holes is searched in order to determine which one should be assigned.

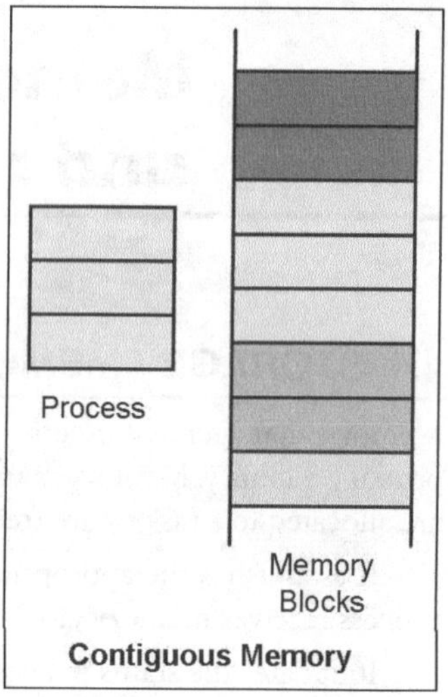

Fig. 4.2.

Non-Contiguous Allocation

- Non-contiguous allocation refers to the ability to allocate noncontiguous memory portions to distinct process components.
- The available memory space is distributed throughout the system rather than concentrated in one location, which is known as non-contiguous memory allocation in relation to memory organization.

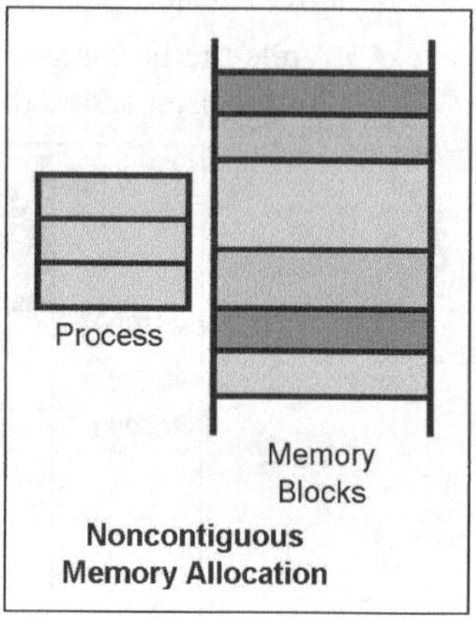

Fig. 4.3.

Contagious Vs Non-Contagious

Contiguous Memory Allocation	Non-Contiguous Memory Allocation
Allocates consecutive blocks of memory to a process.	Allocates separate blocks of memory to a process.
Contiguous memory allocation does not have the overhead of address translation while execution of a process.	Non-contiguous memory allocation has overhead of address translation while execution of a process.
A process executes fatster in contiguous memory allocation	A process executes quite slower complaratively in noncontiguous memory allocation.
The memory space must be divided into the fixed-sized partition and each partition is allocated to a single process only.	Divide the process into several blocks and place them in different parts of the memory according to the availability of memory space available.

4.3 FIXED PARTITION SCHEME

Two partitions may have different sizes, but memory is separated into fixed-size sections.

- Each partition may have a single process.
- The process's maximum size is constrained by the partition's maximum size, and there may be substantial internal fragmentation. Nevertheless, assigning a free partition to a process when it arrives simplifies management.

Scheme For Variable Partition

- A hole is a block of memory that can be used; the memory is surrounded by holes of various sizes.
- When a process arrives, memory is allocated using a hole large enough to accommodate it.

The operating system records information about:

- Allotted partitions
- Free partitions (hole)

4.4 MULTIPROGRAMMING

- To solve the problem of CPU and main memory underutilization, multiprogramming was put into place. When a single computer does multiple jobs sequentially, this is known as multiprogramming.
- While the first program waits for an I/O transfer, another application in a multiprogramming system is ready to access the CPU.
- As a result, sharing the CPU's attention among multiple jobs is possible. It is important to keep in mind that multiprogramming does not imply simultaneous job execution. Rather, it shows that the CPU has access to a large number of jobs (stored in main memory), and that a portion of one work is executed, then another, and so on.

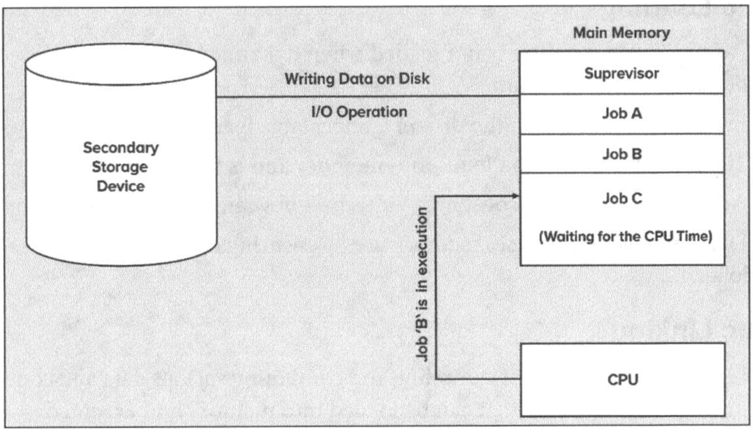

Fig. 4.4.

- In this particular instance, job "A" is not utilizing the CPU time because it is involved in I/O activities.

- Consequently, job 'B' is taking up the CPU. Another job, C, is waiting on the CPU to decide when to run. Because of this, the CPU will never be idle in this scenario and will always be in use.
- A program that is going on is called a "Process," "Job," or "Task."
- Concurrent program execution optimizes resource usage and boosts system throughput in contrast to batch and serial processing.
- This method allocates CPU time to a ready process whenever a process requests I/O allocation.
- As a result, when a process transitions to an I/O task, the CPU is not left idle.
- Multiprogramming is a well-liked resource management technique.
- The core components of an operating system intended for a single user are a file system, a command processor, an input/output control system, and a temporary area.
- Building upon this framework, a multiprogramming operating system separates the temporary space to support numerous independent programs and incorporates resource management processes into the operating system's fundamental functionalities.

Storage Hierarchy

- The wide range of storage choices available in a computer system can be ranked according to speed and cost.
- The more complex stages are quick but expensive. As we move down the hierarchy, the cost per bit decreases, but the access time increases.
- Since magnetic tape and semiconductor memory have become faster and more economical, many early storage systems, like paper tape and core memories, are now only found in museums. Slower memory devices are utilized because they are less expensive than faster ones.

Dynamic Loading

- A program's procedure is not loaded when dynamic loading is employed; it must be called by the program.
- Each routine is kept on the disk in a relocatable load format.
- The primary application loads into memory and is then launched.
- Additional modules, procedures, or techniques can be loaded upon request.
- Dynamic loading reduces memory use by ensuring that unused routines are never loaded.

Dynamic Linking

- Linking is the process of compiling and combining various data and code modules into an executable file that can be loaded into memory and executed.
- The operating system can connect programs to system-level libraries.
- Static linking happens when the libraries are linked together during load time, whereas dynamic linking happens while the program is running.

Logical Vs Physical Address Space

- A logical address is one that is generated by the CPU, whereas a physical address is one that is physically located on the memory unit.
- A virtual address is another term for a logical address.
- The same virtual and physical addresses are used by address-binding techniques that are load-time and compile-time.
- There are differences in the execution-time address-binding method used for virtual and physical addresses.

Table 4.1 *: Logical vs Physical Address*

S.No.	Logical Address	Physical Address
1.	It is the virtual address generated by CPU.	The physical address is a location in a memory unit.
2.	Set of all logical addresses generated by CPU in reference to a program is referred as Logical Address Space.	set of all physical addresses mapped to the corresponding logical addresses is referred as Physical Address.
3.	The user can view the logical address of a program.	The user can never view physical address of program.
4.	The user uses the logical address to access the physical address.	The user can not directly access physical address.
5.	The Logical Address is generated by the CPU.	Physical Address is Computed by MMU.

Swapping

- A technique called swapping allows a process to be momentarily transferred from main memory to a backing store before being returned to memory to continue executing.
- A backing store is typically a hard drive or another type of secondary storage that

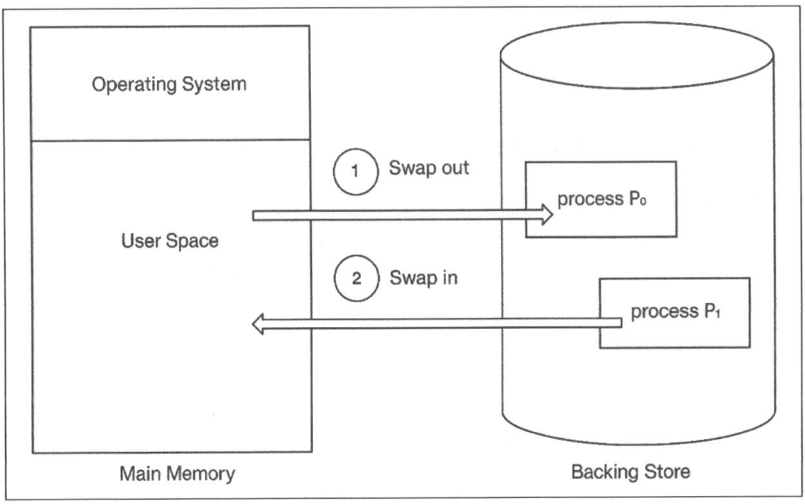

Fig. 4.5.

is quick to access and big enough to hold copies of every memory image for every user.

- It must enable users to access these memory images directly.
- Transfer time is a significant time-consuming aspect of exchanging.
- There is a direct correlation between the amount of memory swapped and the overall transfer time.
- Assume that a normal hard drive with a transfer rate of 1 MB per second serves as the backing store and that the user process is 100 KB in size.
- 100KB / 1000KB per second = 1/10 second = 100 milliseconds

Multiple-Partition Allocation

(A) Fixed Partition Allocation

- One method of allocating memory is to create several fixed-size memory partitions.
- Each division may use the same procedure. Thus, the extent of multiprogramming is limited by the number of divisions.
- When a free partition becomes available, a process selected from the input queue is loaded into it, and the partition is made available for.

(B) Dynamic Allocation

- The operating system maintains a database that shows which memory regions—referred to as holes—are occupied and which are available.
- Initially, there is a single, big hole in the memory that user processes can access.
- We choose a hole that is big enough to accommodate the procedure when it arrives.
- We allocate as much RAM as the process requires, with the remaining space remaining available for future requests. One can select a hole to contain a process using the following algorithms.

First-Fit

- Choose the first sufficiently large hole.
- The search might begin at the beginning of the hole set or at the end of the last.

First-fit Search

- The operating system starts at the beginning of primary memory and allocates memory from the first hole it finds big enough to fulfill the request in order to cut down on the amount of time it spends examining the available spaces because there may be several holes in the memory.

Best-Fit

- Select the smallest hole that is sufficiently large. Unless the list is kept arranged by size, we have to search the entire thing.
- The smallest remaining hole is created by this method.

Worst-Fit

- Allocate Unless the list is arranged by size, we must scan the entire list and assign the largest hole that is large enough.
- This tactic leaves the biggest hole behind. According to the theory, this arrangement will result in the greatest hold following the allocations, increasing the likelihood that a different process could utilize the remaining space instead of best fit.

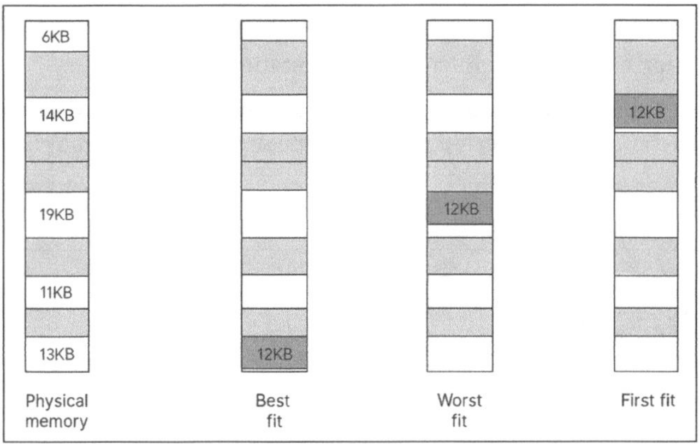

Fig. 4.6.

Fragmentation

- As processes are loaded and discharged, the free memory space is split up into little pieces. Sometimes memory blocks are left idle because processes cannot be allocated to them due to their small size. This problem is known as fragmentation.
- This can also mean that a computer user is constantly loading and unloading processes from main memory. Blocks of main memory are where processes are kept. Fragmentation is the state that occurs when there are some free memory blocks but not enough to load the process.
- Fragmentation is a state that arises when processes dynamically allocate RAM to one another, leaving numerous free memory blocks accessible but insufficient to load the process onto RAM.

Types

- External fragmentation
- Internal fragmentation

1. External Fragmentation

- When a dynamic memory allocation mechanism distributes some memory and a tiny amount.
- The free memory space is divided into tiny fragments as processes are loaded and released. Because memory blocks are so small, processes are often unable to allocate them, leaving them idle. We call this issue fragmentation.
- Additionally, it may indicate that a user is continuously loading and unloading programs from main memory. Processes are stored in blocks of main memory.

When there are some free memory blocks but not enough to load the process, the state known as fragmentation takes place.

- When processes dynamically distribute RAM to one another, a condition known as fragmentation occurs, leaving many free memory blocks available but not enough to load the process onto RAM.

2. Internal Fragmentation

- The waste of space within memory blocks that are allocated as a result of block size restrictions is known as internal fragmentation.
- Memory that is part of a partition but not being used may be represented by a mismatch between allocated and requested memory, which may be slightly greater.

4.5 PAGING

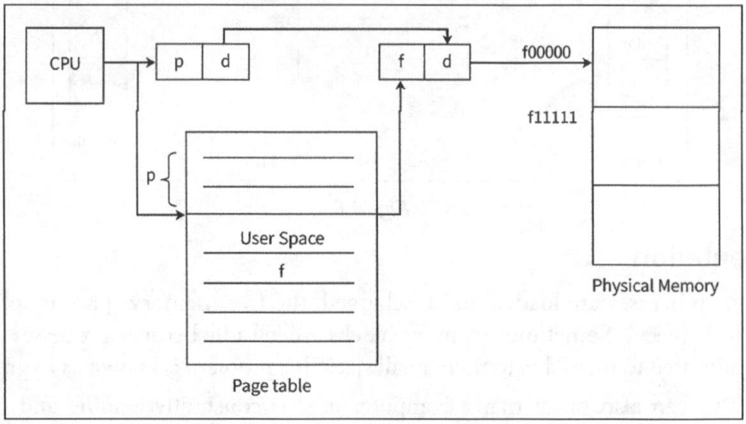

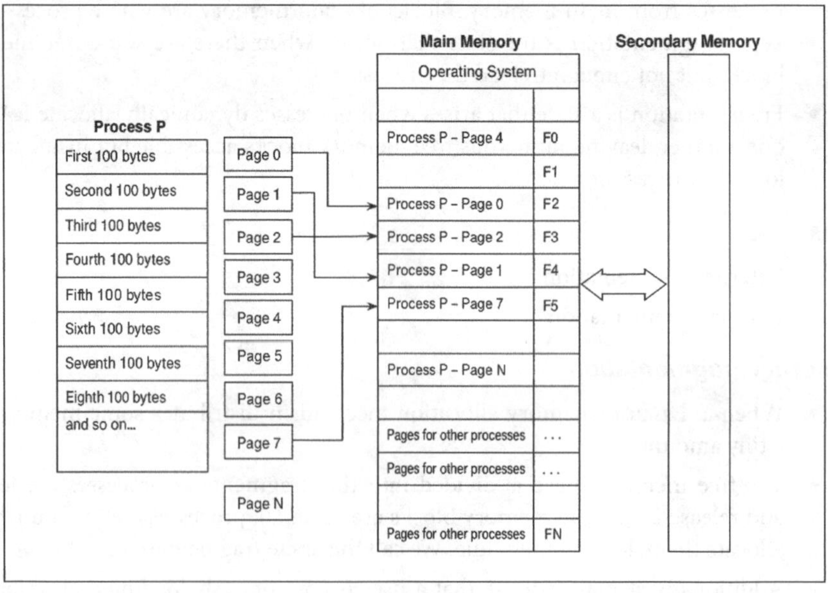

Fig. 4.7.

- Physical memory can no longer be allocated in a contiguous fashion thanks to paging.
- With this architecture, the physical address space of a process might not be contiguous.
- The logical or virtual address, which is expressed in bits, is created by the CPU.
- The "logical address space" or "virtual address space," which can be represented in words or bytes, is the collection of all logical addresses in a program.
- Bit-by-bit representation of the physical address: The memory unit's actual physical address
- The physical address space, represented in words or bytes, is the set of all physical addresses that correspond to the logical addresses.
- Physical memory is composed of fixed-size blocks called frames. Furthermore, logical memory is separated into PAGES, or blocks of the same size.
- Pages from the backup store are loaded into any available memory frames when a process is ready to run. As a result, a process's pages might not be consecutive.

Address Translation

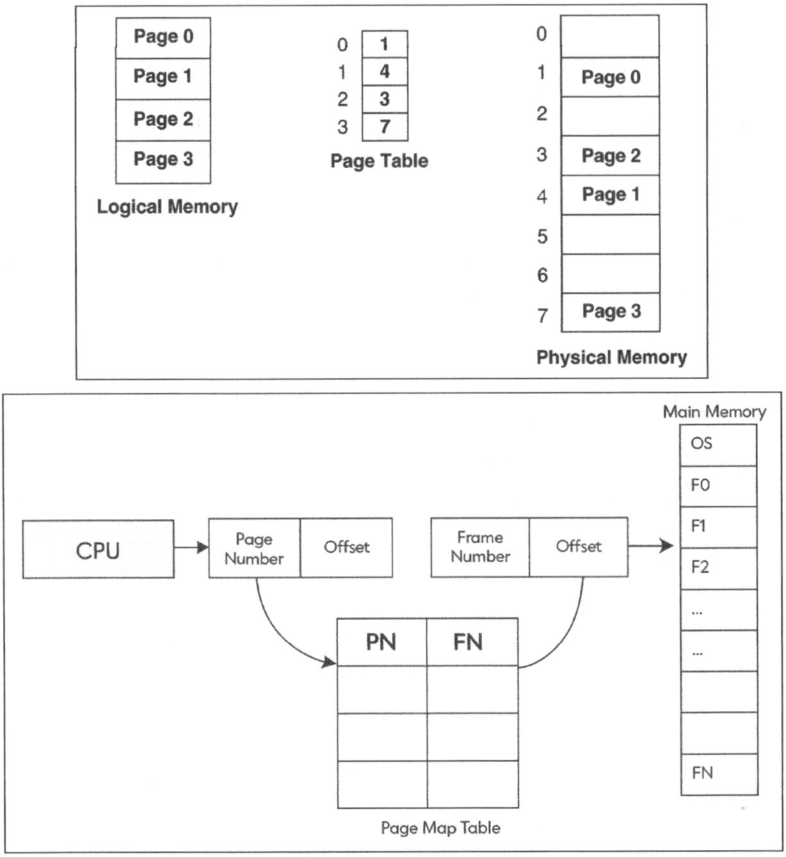

Fig. 4.8.

- Page address is called logical address and represented by page number and the offset.
  - Logical Address = Page number + page offset
- Fram address is called Physical address and represented by a frame number and the offset.
  - Physical Address = Frame number + page offset
- Paging eliminates external fragmentation altogethr but there may be a little internal fragmentation.

Advantages And Disadvantages Of Paging

- While paging reduces external fragmentation, internal fragmentation still happens.
- Paging is thought to be a user-friendly and efficient memory management strategy.
- It is easy to flip between pages and frames because they are the same size.
- Because page tables require more memory, they might not function properly on computers with low RAM.

Multilevel Paging

- Most computer systems offer large logical address spaces (between 232 and 264). In this case, the page table itself becomes rather large.
- As an example, consider a 32-bit logical address area. If a page contains 4K bytes (212), then a table may contain up to (232 / 212) = 1 million items. If each entry is 4 bytes long, each process may need 4 GB of physical address simply for the page table.
- Because page tables may have millions of items each, they have the drawback of consuming a large amount of physical memory.

Inverted Page Table

- An inverted page table could be used to get around the drawbacks of the page tables mentioned To overcome the limitations of the aforementioned page tables, an inverted page table could be utilized.
- A single entry in an inverted page table corresponds to each memory frame.

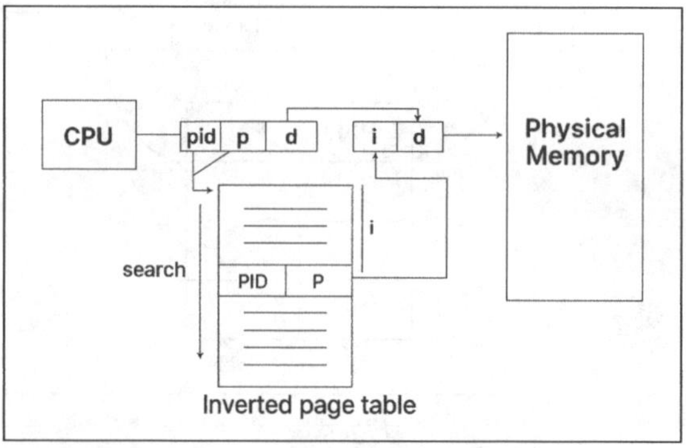

Fig. 4.9.

Disadvantage

- A disadvantage is that it no longer saves all of the information about a process's logical address space, which is required in case a referred page is now out of memory.
- This can be avoided by maintaining an external page table (one for each process). These tables are similar to the traditional per-process page table in that they provide information on the locations of each logical page.
- These external page tables don't have to be in the RAM all the time because they are only needed in case of a page defect.

Protection

In a paged environment, protection bits linked to every frame carry out memory protection. They are often stored in the page table.

- A single bit can specify whether a page is read-only or read-and-write.

Shared Pages

- The ability to share code is an additional benefit of paging.
- Take into consideration a system that can accommodate 40 users, each of whom uses a text editor.
- We would require 8000K to support 40 users if the text editor has 150K of code and 50K of data space.
- The code can be distributed among the 40 users if it is reentrant, or non-self-modifying.

4.6 SEGMENTATION

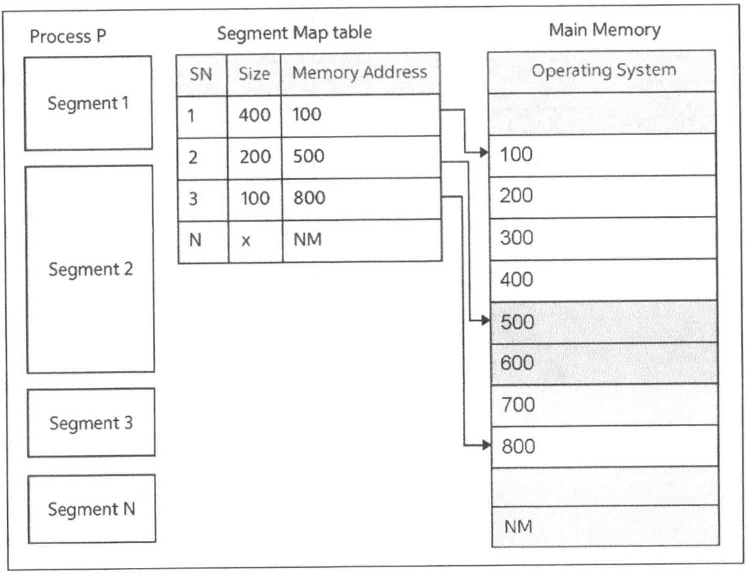

Fig. 4.10.

- Segmentation is a memory management technique that splits each task into numerous, different-sized segments, one for each module made up of parts that perform related activities.
- Each segment actually corresponds to a different logical address area in the program.
- Segmentation memory management works similarly to paging, however paging pages are fixed in size, while segments are changeable in length.
- Although each segment is put into a contiguous block of available memory, the appropriate segmentations of a process are loaded into non-contiguous memory when the process is to be performed.
- A program segment contains data structures, utility functions, and the main purpose of the program.
- A memory-management technique called segmentation proposes splitting a logical address space into a number of segments. Every segment has a length and a name.
- Addresses define the offset inside the segment as well as the segment name.
- As a result, the user specifies each address using two numbers: an offset and a segment name (also known as a segment number).
- SEGMENT NUMBER (S): The segment number serves as an index into a segment table that includes the limit of each segment as well as the base address of each segment in physical memory.
- SEGMENT OFFSET (O): To establish the physical memory address, the segment offset is first compared to the limit and then joined with the base address.

Thus, two tuples make up logical addresses:

The offset and segment-number

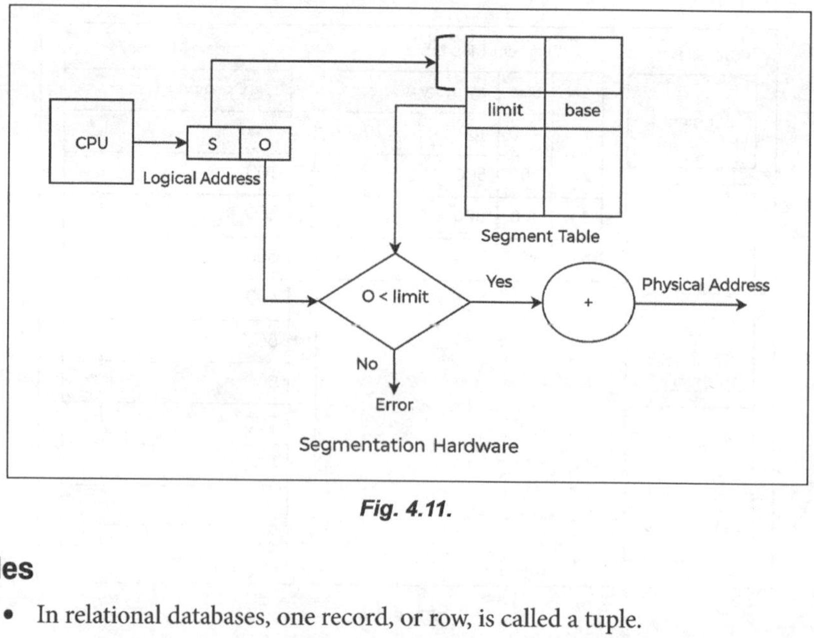

Fig. 4.11.

Tuples

- In relational databases, one record, or row, is called a tuple.

- Consider the data in a database as a spreadsheet, with columns (also known as fields or attributes) representing different types of data and tuples (rows) representing all the data from each field associated with a single record.

Segmentation Hardware

- Every segment table entry has a segment base and segment limit. The segment base represents the segment's initial physical address in main memory, whilst the segment limit denotes the segment's length.
- The main difference between segmentation and multi-partition systems is that a single program can have multiple segments, and the segment table can be kept in fast registers or memory.
- When a program contains multiple segments that need to be stored in memory, a segmenttable base register (STBR) is required to point to the segment table.
- Additionally, because the number of segments in a program can vary widely, a segment-table length register (STLR) is required.
- One advantage of segmentation is that memory is automatically secured because of the segment-table entries (base and limit tuples).
- Segments may also be shared in a system with segmented memory. Segmentation may lead to external fragmentation.

Paged-Segmentation

A memory management approach called "paged segmentation" splits the address space of a process into segments, which are then further subdivided into pages. This makes it possible for memory to be allocated in a flexible way, with various sizes for each segment and pages inside segments.

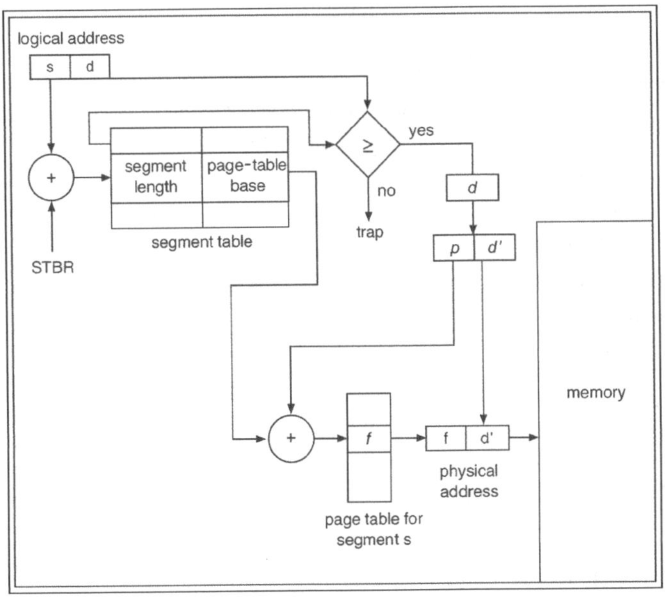

Fig. 4.12.

Multics

We now take the example of one of the finest operating systems of late 1960s and early 1970s, known as the MULTICS operating system. Here are the specifications of the CPU supported by MULTICS and calculation of its various parameters such as the largest segment size supported by MULTICS.

- GE 345 processor
- Logical address = 34 bits

Advantages of Segmentation

- **Flexibility:** Segmentation provides a higher degree of flexibility than paging. Segments can be of variable size, and processes can be designed to have multiple segments, allowing for more fine-grained memory allocation.
- **Sharing:** Segmentation allows for sharing of memory segments between processes. This can be useful for inter-process communication or for sharing code libraries.
- **Protection:** Segmentation provides a level of protection between segments, preventing one process from accessing or modifying another process's memory segment. This can help increase the security and stability of the system.

Disadvantage of Segmentation

- Overhead is associated with keeping a segment table for each activity.
- Due to the need for two memory accesses, one for the segment table and the other for main memory, access time to retrieve the instruction increases.
- **Fragmentation:** As mentioned, segmentation can lead to external fragmentation as memory becomes divided into smaller segments. This can lead to wasted memory and decreased performance.

4.7 PAGE REPLACEMENT

- In order to decide which page should be replaced when a new page is inserted, operating systems that employ paging for memory management need page replacement algorithms.
- Whenever a new page is requested but not located in memory, the operating system substitutes a newly needed page for one of the existing pages.
- Different page replacement algorithms provide different approaches for figuring out which page has to be changed.
- Every technique aims to reduce the number of page faults.

Page Fault

When a running application accesses a memory page that is mapped into the virtual address space but not stored in physical memory, the hardware raises a page fault, a form of interrupt.

Page Replacement Algorithms

- There are numerous algorithms for replacing pages. The replacement algorithm with the lowest page-fault rate is the one we choose.

- To assess an algorithm, it is performed on a specific string of memory accesses, known as a reference string, and the number of page faults is calculated.
- access strings can be created automatically (for instance, by monitoring a system and noting the address of each memory access) or by using a random-number generator.

Types Of Replacement Algorithms

- FIFO – First In First Out
- LRU – Least Recently Used
- Optimal Algorithm
- LFU -Least Frequently Used
- MFU -Least Frequently Used

Page Replacement Algorithms

- The Longest time period repeated page are to be replaced first.
- **Page Fault:** The CPU will demand for particular page number: If it is not present in reference string (RAM/main memory). Then it is going to be Page Fault.
- **Page Hit:** The CPU will demand for the particular page number; If it is present in the RAM/main memory. Then it is goin to be Page Hit.

Types: → **FIFO:** First In First Out.
→ **LRU:** Least Recently Used.
→ **Optimal Algorithm.**

} with the help of these 3, we can find Page Fault, Page Hit, Hit ratio.

FIFO

- First In First Out
- From the name itself we can recognize that which page has to be replaced first and which page has to be deleted first.
- Replace the pages that has been in the RAM/main memory for the longest time period.
- The Example as follows,

Reference string:

7 0 1 2 0 3 0 4 2 3 0 3 1 2 0

- These page numbers are present in the RAM/memory
- Because the main memory size is lesson than the logical memory.
- The main memory can't store all the pages at a time.
- If the particular demanded page number not present in main memory. It has to be borrowed from secondary memory, by deleting the longest time repeated page number.
- If the page faults are more than RAM gets slower.

Page frames	7	0	1	2	0	3	0	4	2	3	0	3	1	2	0
F_1	(7)	7	7	(2)	2	2	2	(4)	4	4	0	0	0	0	Present 0
F_2		(0)	0	Present 0	0	(3)	3	3	(2)	2	2	2	1	1	1
F_3			(1)	1	1	1	(0)	0	0	(3)	3	Present 3	3	2	2
	*	*	*	*	Hit	*	*	*	*	*	*	Hit	*	*	Hit

Page Hit: **Hits** → 3

Page faults: * → 12

Reference string → 15

Explanation for FIFO:

- Starting RAM/main memory is free. It does not contains any page number.
- It contains (RAM) only three frames for replacing the longest time period page number.
- The CPU is demanding for page no. 7..

The RAM doesn't contains any page no. in the starting. So CPU will borrow the particular page number from RAM. So page no. 7 is not there in RAM. Then it is going to be 'Page fault *'

- The process continous like this...
- Now the CPU is demanding for page '0'.

↓

7 0 1 2 **0** 3 0 4 2 3 0 3 1 2 0

↓

⇒ It is present in the given Reference String. Then it is going to be 'Page Hit – **Hit**'.

$$\text{Hit ratio} = \frac{\text{No. of Hits}}{\text{Total no. of Reference string}} = \frac{3}{15} \times 10 = 20\% \text{ (approx)}$$

$$\text{Page fault} = \frac{\text{No. of fault}}{\text{Ref. string}} = \frac{12}{15} \times 100 = 80\% \text{ (approx)}$$

- Now, check the frame: 4 0 2 and page number (0 4 2). In frames 2 is very most recently used: 4 is mostly recently used (only 2 times repeated. We should replace the frame with another page number only if particular page number repeats 3 & above times). So in this condition you just delete the frame (F_2) – '0' with '3'.

The process continuous...

Page Hit = 3

Page Fault = 12

Optimal Algorithm:

- This algorithm represents the longest time period page number in future (Right Direction).

Example:

Longest time in Future →

7	0	1	2	0	3	0	4	2	3	0	3	2	1	2	0	1	7
7	7	(7)	2	2	2	2	2	2	2	2	2	2	2	2	2	(2)	7
	0	0	0	0	(0)	4	4	(4)	0	0	0	0	0	0	0	0	(7)
		1	1	(1)	3	3	3	3	3	3	3	(3)	1	1	1	1	1
*	*	*	*	Hit	*	Hit	*	Hit	Hit	*	Hit	Hit	*	Hit	Hit	Hit	*

Explanation:

- The process stark as usual;

LRU

- Least Recently Used.
- Note: 3 Frames = 3 page numbers. (compare)
- Left side page numbers are replaced with another.

Example:

(consider two 0's as one)

7 0 1 2 0 3 0 4 2 3 0 3 1 2 0

(consider two 3's as one)

	7	0	1	2	0	3	0	4	2	3	0	3	1	2	0
F_1	7	7	(7)	2	2	2	(2)	4	4	(4)	0	0	(0)	2	2
F_2		0	0	0	0	0	0	0	(0)	3	3	3	3	(3)	0
F_3			1	1	(1)	3	3	(3)	2	2	2	(2)	1	1	1
	*	*	*	*	Hit	*	Hit	*	*	*	*	Hit	*	*	*

- Step 1: 7 0 1 (frame) = 7 0 1 (page no.). check the arrow [For your Reference]
- Step 2: compare the page numbers and frames in left direction.
- Don't compare the Frame F2 for the particular time period.
- Check the frames with given page numbers.

For example: 7 0 1 (1 is most recently used. 7 is Least recently used, so select '7' and replace with next page number '2').

The process continuous...

- Now, check for longest time in future.

⇒ 7 0 1 (frames); comparing these numbers in given Reference string. 7 is most longest traveled page number (i.e., Repeated in future).

These processes continues...

- Now, page number 4 is not there in future reference string. In this condition, just replace the longest time repeated frame with another page number (i.e) '0' is replaced with 4.

- Then process repeats. After that 4 is not there in future reference string. So if it is in frames also no use. So just delete that page number and replace '0'.
- 2 (4) 3 replace with 2 0 3
- The process continuous. Last 7 is not there in future. So just replace with longest traveled page number (2) with 7.

Page Hit -9.

Page fault -9.

LFU (Least Frequently Used) Algorithm

- The algorithm known as LFU (Least Frequently Used)
- Change the page that isn't used as much.

Drawbacks:

- This method has trouble with the scenario when a page is highly used in the beginning of a process but is never used thereafter
- Even if it is no longer required, it has a high count and is still stored in memory because of its extensive use.

MFU (Least Frequently Used) Algorithm

- The algorithm known as MFU (Least Frequently Used)
- Change the page that is used the most.

Drawback:

- This algorithm is predicated on the notion that the page with the lowest count was most likely freshly added and hasn't been used yet.
- Replacement of either MFU or LFU is uncommon.

Virtual Memory

- Virtual memory is a technique that allows the execution of processes that may not be completely in memory.
- A program may frequently never execute all of its components during operation; virtual memory is a mechanism that enables the execution of processes that might not be entirely in memory.
- Logical memory and physical memory are separated into virtual memory. Demand paging is frequently used to implement virtual memory.
- It can be used in a segmentation system as well.
- The following are some benefits of virtual memory:
  - Programs with a logical address space larger than the physical address space could be written by users.
  - The degree of multiprogramming could be increased by running more applications concurrently.
  - Each user software would operate more quickly since less I/O would be required to load or swap it into memory.

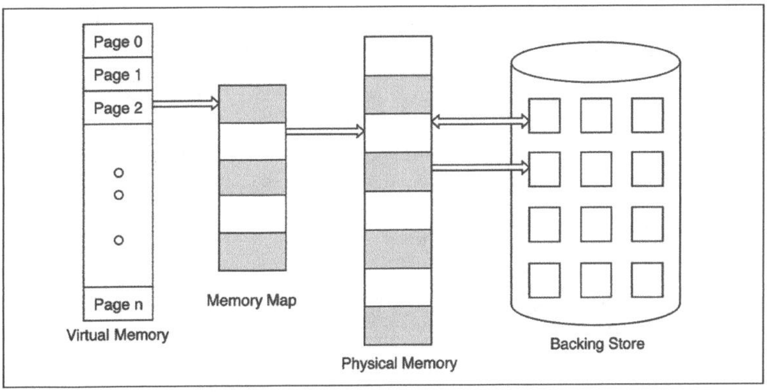

Fig. 4.13.

4.8 DEMAND PAGING

- A demand-paging system is similar to a paging system with swapping.
- When a process is ready to be switched in, the pager anticipates which pages will be used before it is switched out again.
- By avoiding reading into memory pages that won't be used anyway, the pager minimizes the amount of physical memory needed and the swap time by simply bringing the pages that are needed into the memory rather than swapping in a complete process.

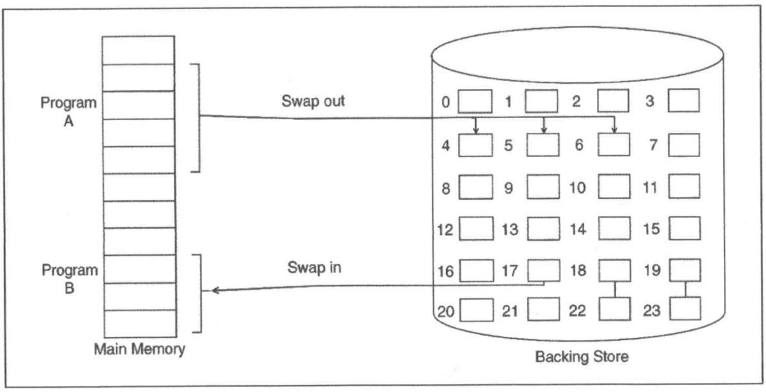

***Fig.4.14:** Demand Paging*

- To distinguish between pages in memory and those on disk, we use an invalid-valid bit, a field in each page-table entry.
- When this bit is set to "valid," it indicates that the associated page is both authentic and stored in memory.
- If the bit is set to "invalid," the page is either genuine but still on the disk or invalid (i.e., not in the process's logical address space).
- The page-table entry for a page that is currently out of memory is either simply marked as invalid or contains the disk address of the page.

- When a page that has been marked as invalid is accessed, a page-fault trap happens. To fix a page fault, perform these steps:

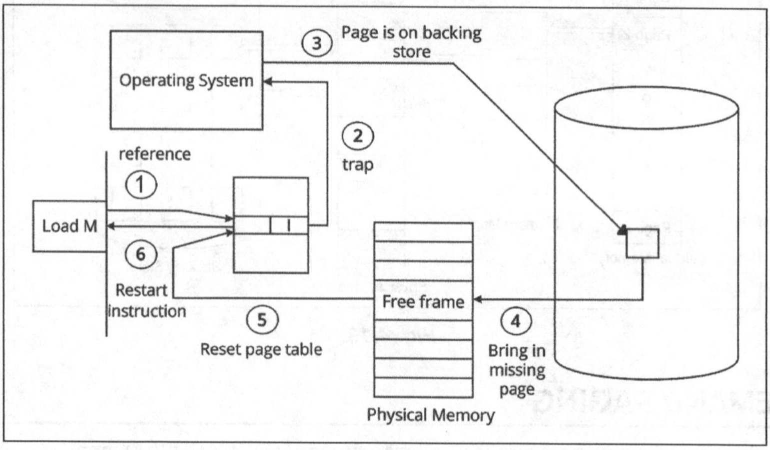

Fig.4.15.

Advantages

- Greater memory efficiency.
- Unrestricted multiprogramming.
- Large virtual memory.
- The degree of multiprogramming has no upper limit.

Disadvantages

- Because jobs address space size is not explicitly constrained, the number of tables and processor overhead for managing page interruptions are higher than in the case of the simple paged management solutions.

Pure Demand Paging

In the worst case scenario, we could start a process with no memory pages.

If the operating system placed the instruction pointer to the process's first instruction on a page that doesn't contain memory, the process would fault for the page right away.

4.8.1 Demand Paging Vs Anticipatory Paging

Demand Paging

- The system loads a page from secondary storage into main memory only when the process specifically accesses it; otherwise, it loads the page containing the process's initial instruction into main memory when the process first starts.
- Needs a procedure to gather pages one at a time.

Anticipatory Paging

- Anticipatory paging solutions must be carefully planned to ensure that the overhead they impose does not impair system performance.
- The operating system tries to anticipate the pages a process will require and preloads these pages when memory space is available.

4.9 FILE CONCEPT

A file is a named collection of related information that is recorded on secondary storage. Data can NOT be written to secondary storage unless they are within a file.

Structure of File

- A text file is a collection of characters organized in lines.
- A group of functions and subroutines is called a source file.
- A group of bytes organized in blocks that the system's linker can understand is called an object file.
- An executable file is a collection of code segments that may be loaded into memory and executed by the loader.

File Structure

- A string of characters arranged in lines is called a text file.
- A source file is a collection of functions and subroutines.
- An object file is a collection of bytes arranged in blocks that the system's linker can comprehend.
- A sequence of code segments that the loader may bring into memory and run is known as an executable file.

File Attributes

- Name: only information kept in human-readable form
- Type: required for systems that allow several types
- Identifier: a unique tag (number) that identifies a file within a file system
- Name: only information maintained in a human-readable manner
- Time, date, and user identification are data for security, protection, and usage monitoring
- Location is a pointer to the file location on the device; size is the current file size
- Protection is a control over who can read, write, and execute; and information about files is stored in the directory structure, which is kept on the disk.

File Operations

To create, write, read, move, delete, and truncate files, the operating system offers system calls. For each of these fundamental file actions, we examine what the operating system needs to do.

1. Creating A File

The file must first find space in the file system. Second, the directory needs to be updated with the new file. The directory entry keeps track of the file's name and system location.

2. Writing A File

The file name and the data to be written to the file must be specified in the system call for writing in a file. To locate the file, the operating system looks through the directory.

A write pointer to the file location where the subsequent write is to occur is stored by the system. Every time a write is made, the write pointer needs to be changed.

3. Reading A File

To read a file, we issue a system call with the file's name and the location (in memory) of the file's subsequent block.

Similar to writing, the system looks through the directory to locate the file and stores a read pointer to the file's location where the subsequent read should occur.

Every time a read takes place, the read pointer needs to be changed.

4. Repositioning Within A File

This operation sets the current-file-position o to a specified value after searching the directory for the named file. We refer to this file activity as a FILE SEEK.

5. Deleting A File

We look through the directory to find the relevant entry. After locating it, we remove the directory entry and free up all the space that the file has occupied.

6. Truncating A File

This function is employed when a user wishes to remove a file's contents while maintaining its properties.

4.9.1 Memory-Mapped Files

- Some operating systems allow file segments to be mapped into memory on virtual memory systems.
- It makes it possible to logically link a section of a file to a section of the virtual address space. By treating reads and writes to that memory space as reads and writes to the file, this significantly streamlines the use of files. When a file is closed, all of the memory-mapped data is removed from the process's virtual memory and copied back to the disk.

Open Files

- **File pointer:** the last read/write location for the file, according to the process that is currently using it.
- **File-open count:** on the final close, the counter that counts openings and closes approaches zero. The entry can then be deleted by the system.
- **The file's disk location:** the details required to find the file on disk.
- **Access rights:** details on the per-process access mode that the OS uses to approve or reject a subsequent I/O request

File Types – Name, Extension

File Type	Usual Extension	Function
executable	exe, com, bin or none	ready-to-run machine language program

File Type	Usual Extension	Function
object	obj, o	compiled, machine language, not linked
source code	c, cc, java, pas, asm, a	source code in various languages
batch	bat, sh	commands to the command interpreter
text	txt, doc	textual data, documents
word processor	wp, tex, rtf, doc	various word-processor formats
library	lib, a, so, dll	libraries of routines for programmers
print or view	ps, pdf, jpg	ASCII or binary file in a format for printing or viewing
archive	arc, zip, tar	related files grouped into one file, sometimes compressed, for archiving or storage
multimedia	mpeg, mov, rm, mp3, avi	binary file containing audio or A/V information

File Concepts and Types

Access Methods

- Sequential Access

read next
write next
reset
no read after last write
(rewrite)

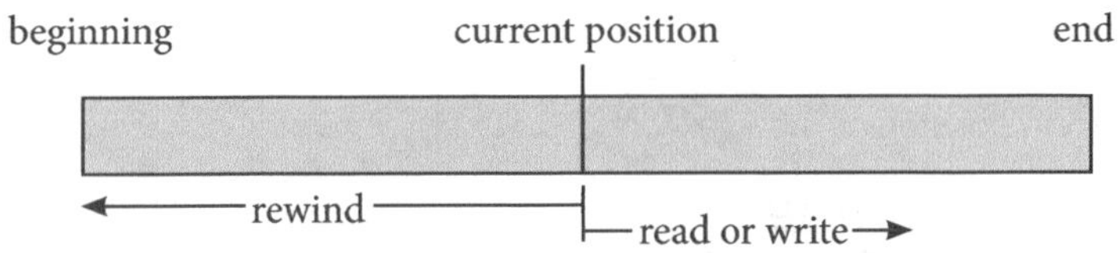

- Direct Access

read n
write n
position to n
read next
write next
rewrite n
n = relative block number

Index and Relative Files

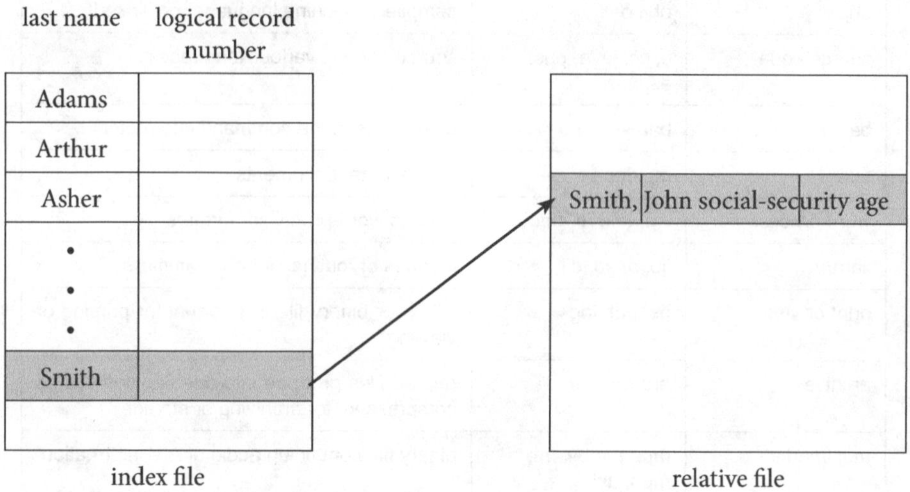

- The index contains pointers to the various blocks.
- To find a record in the file, we first search the index and then use the pointer to access the file directly and to find the desired record.

Simulation of Sequential Access on Direct-access File

Sequential access	Implementation for direct access
reset	cp = 0
read next	read cp; cp = cp + 1;
write next	write cp; cp = cp + 1;

CP ⇒ current position

4.10 DISK STRUCTURE

- The disk can have partitions made on it. One kind of disk or partition that is protected against failure is called a Redundant Array of Independent Disks (RAID).
- Partitions, also known as minidisks or slices, can be utilized unformatted or formatted using a file system.
- A file system is contained in an entity known as a volume.
- Information about a file system is also recorded in the device directory or volume table of contents for each volume that contains it.

There are five commonly used directory structures:

- Single-Level Directory
- Two-Level Directory

- Tree-Structure Directories
- Acyclic-Graph Directories
- General Graph Directories

Operations Performed on Directory:

- Search for a file
- Create a file
- Delete a file
- List a directory
- Rename a file
- Traverse the file system

A Typical File-System Organization

The traditional head-sector-cylinder, or HSC, numbers are translated to linear block addresses by identifying the first sector on the first head on the outermost track as sector 0. Numbering begins with the remaining sectors on the same track and then on to the other tracks on the same cylinder before proceeding to the center of the disk via the remaining cylinders. In contemporary usage, these linear block addresses are used instead of the HSC numbers for several reasons.

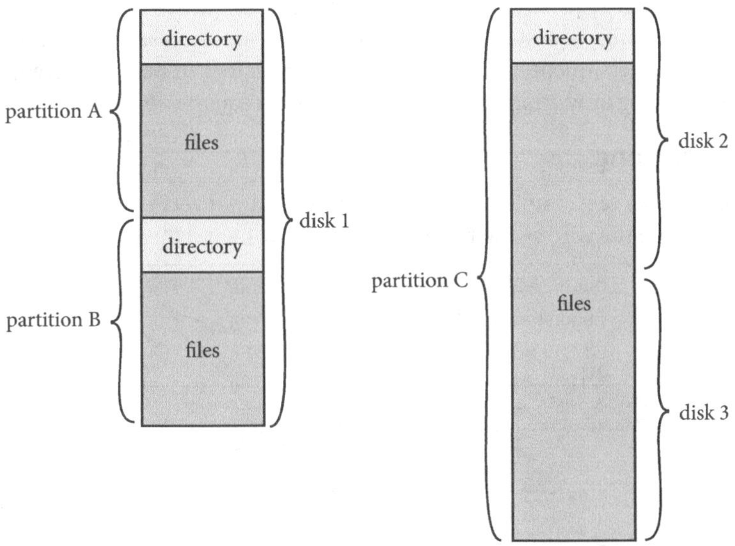

1. Because the linear length of the tracks on the disk's outside edge is substantially longer than that of the tracks near its core, many more sectors can fit onto outer tracks than onto inner ones.
2. Since every disk contains some faulty sectors, disks maintain a few spare sectors that can be used in place of the damaged ones. The mapping of spare sectors to bad sectors is managed internally by the disk controller.
3. Since every disk contains some faulty sectors, disks store a few spare sectors that can be used in place of the damaged ones. The mapping of spare sectors to bad sectors is managed internally by the disk controller.

4. Thousands of cylinders and hundreds of sectors can be found in the outermost tracks of modern hard disks. Since these numbers are higher than the range of HSC numbers for many (earlier) operating systems, disks can be made to accommodate any feasible combination of HSC values that fall within the total number of sectors physically present on the drive.

The degree to which individual bits may be ordered on physical media is limited, although it is getting closer and closer as technology advances. Modern disks fit a lot more sectors onto outside cylinders than inner ones using one of two techniques:

- Constant Linear Velocity, or CLV, ensures that bit density remains constant across cylinders. Because outer cylinders have more sectors, the disk spins more slowly when reading them, maintaining a constant bit-moving rate beneath the read-write head. This is the technique used by modern CDs and DVDs.
- When Constant Angular Velocity, or CAV, is used, the disk rotates at a constant angular speed but the bit density on the outer cylinders falls.

4.11 DISK SCHEDULING

As previously stated, search times and rotational latency are the main factors limiting disk transfer speeds. Waiting for additional requests to be processed adds an inherent delay when processing numerous requests. The quantity of data transported divided by the entire time from the initial request to the last transfer (for a sequence of disk requests) is the bandwidth. Processing requests in a suitable sequence can increase bandwidth and access time. The disk address, memory address, number of sectors to be transferred, and if the request is for reading or writing are all included in disk requests.

FCFS Scheduling

First-Come First-Serve is simple and intrinsically fair, but not very efficient. Consider in the following sequence the wild swing from cylinder 122 to 14 and then back to 124:

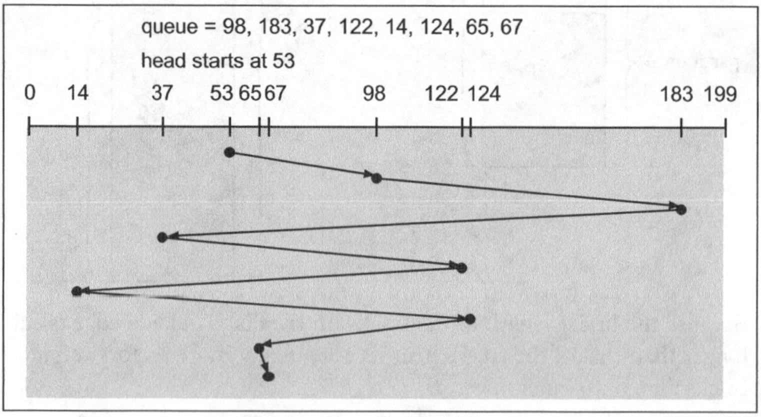

Fig.4.16: FCFS disk scheduling

SSTF Scheduling

Shortest Seek Time (SSTF) Scheduling Although first scheduling is more effective, it could cause starvation if a steady flow of requests for the same general disk location keeps coming in. The total head movement needed for the identical set of queries under FCFS is reduced to 236 cylinders under SSTF. However, keep in mind that by processing the first 37 and then 14 requests before moving on to the remaining requests, the distance might be further decreased to 208.

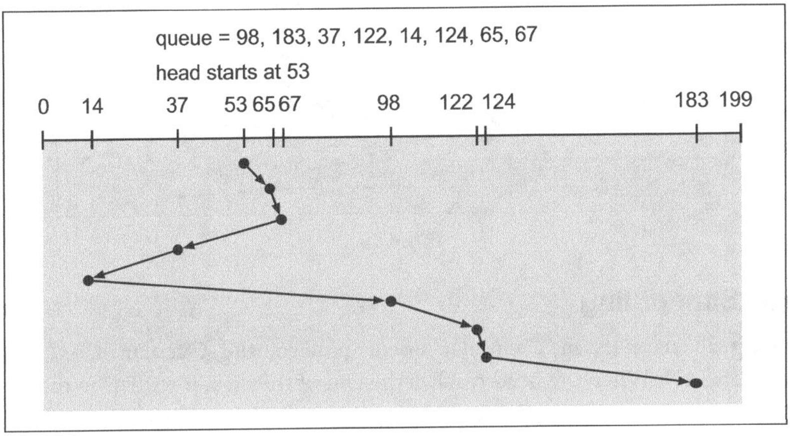

Fig.4.17.

SCAN Scheduling

The SCAN algorithm, a.k.a. the elevator algorithm moves back and forth from one end of the disk to the other, similarly to an elevator processing requests in a tall building.

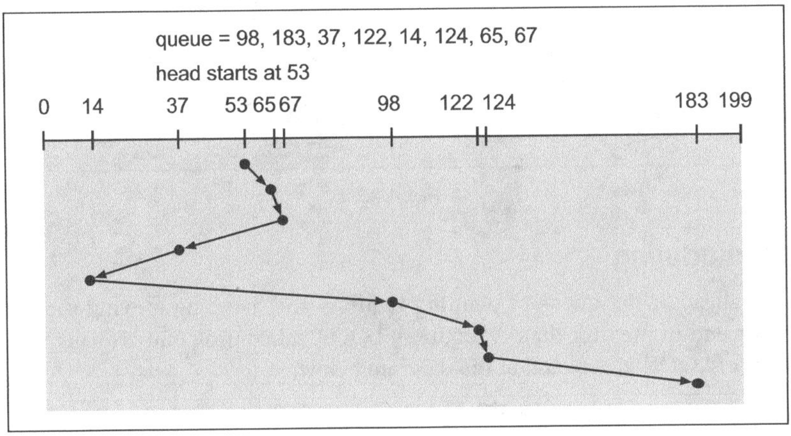

Fig.4.18.

SCAN Disk Scheduling

A request will be handled immediately if it comes in front of the moving head according to the SCAN algorithm; if it comes in after the head has passed, it will have to wait for the head to pass in the opposite direction on the return trip. This results in a rather large range of access times that could be reduced. Take the following scenario, for instance, when the head hits the disk's high end: While requests with low numbers might have been waiting for a lot longer, those with high cylinder numbers just missed the passing head, indicating that they are all relatively recent.

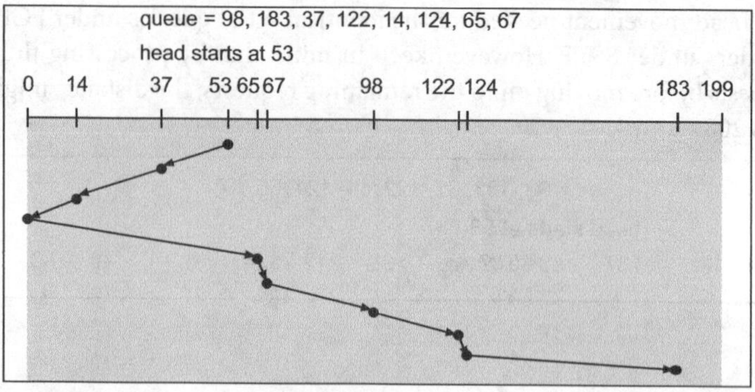

Fig.4.19.

C-SCAN Scheduling

By handling all requests in a circular queue pattern, the Circular-SCAN algorithm outperforms SCAN. When the head reaches the end of the disk, it returns to the other end without processing any requests before starting over at the beginning:

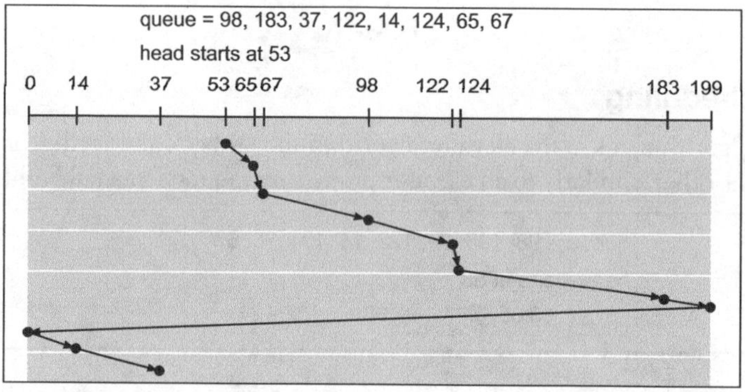

Fig.4.20.

LOOK Scheduling

By looking ahead at the queue of pending requests and avoiding moving the heads any closer to the end of the disk than is required, LOOK scheduling outperforms SCAN. The round form of LOOK is depicted in the diagram below:

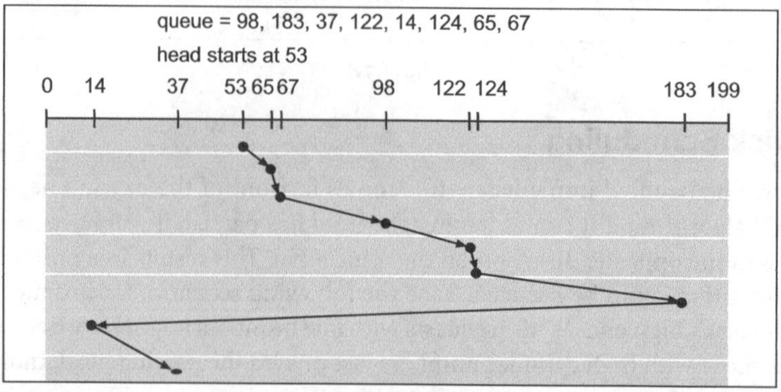

Fig.4.21: *C-LOOK disk scheduling*

Selection of a Disk-Scheduling Algorithm

Under extremely mild loads, all algorithms function identically because there is usually only one request to complete at a time. For slightly higher loads, SSTF outperforms FCFS; nonetheless, it may result in hunger. When the loads' weight is adequate. For busier systems, starvation problems are resolved by the SCAN and LOOK algorithms. The incremental improvements are usually not worth the additional cost, even if the actual optimal approach may be far more complex than the ones shown here. It is possible to strategically arrange directory and/or inode information to maximize overall file system access times.

If those structures are placed in the middle of the disk instead of at the beginning, the maximum distance between them and the data blocks is reduced to just half of the disk size. If those structures can be further distributed and their data blocks are kept as close to the appropriate directory structures as possible, it will take less time overall to find the disk block numbers and then access the pertinent data blocks. The OS is unable to account for the rotational latency, which can be almost as critical as seek time, because modern disks do not reveal their underlying sector mapping methods. When defective blocks have been remapped to spare sectors, this is particularly true. Some disk manufacturers incorporate disk scheduling algorithms directly into their disk controllers to execute a sequence of requests delivered from the computer to the controller in the optimal order. Both the actual geometry of the disk and any remapping are known to these controllers.

Unfortunately, the operating system must consider certain aspects that the on-board disk-scheduling algorithms are unable to manage, such as the need to prioritize certain demands over others or the necessity to execute particular requests in a particular order. Operating systems may therefore choose to spoon-feed requests to the disk controller one at a time in specific situations.

4.12 DISK MANAGEMENT: DISK FORMATTING

Before a disk can be used, it must be low-level formatted, which means that all of the headers and trailers that indicate the beginning and ending of each sector must be written down. The linear sector numbers and error-correcting codes (ECC) found in the header and trailer allow for the identification of damaged sectors and, depending on the extent of the damage, the recovery of the lost data. Larger drives may have larger sectors, even though the normal sector size is 512 bytes.

Every disk read or write is subjected to an ECC calculation; if damage is found but the data may be recovered, a soft error has taken place. The OS never sees soft faults, which are often handled by the on-board disk controller. (See below.) Partitioning the drive into one or more distinct partitions comes after the disk has been low-level formatted. In order for the partition table to be written to the beginning of the disk, this step needs to be finished even if the disk is going to be utilized as a single huge partition. After partitioning, the file systems must be logically formatted, which comprises initializing free lists, establishing the root directory, and entering the master directory information (inode structure or FAT table). Logical formatting is absent from disk partitions meant for use as raw devices. The application program still has to manage its own disk storage requirements even when the overhead and disk space of the file system structure are reduced.)

Boot Block

Only the code necessary to find the first hard drive sector on the first controller, load that sector into memory, and transfer control to it is present in a bootstrap program (OS independent) in computer ROM. (The ROM bootstrap program may scan floppy and/or CD drives before accessing the hard drive, and it is smart enough to know whether it has found a valid boot code or not.) Apart from the partition table, the first sector on the hard drive is called the Master Boot Record, or MBR, and it has very little code in it. The partition table describes how the disk is partitioned into logical disks and indicates which partition is the boot or active partition. After that, the boot software searches the active partition for an operating system, sometimes loading a somewhat bigger or more complex boot program in the process. The user may be able to select which operating system to boot on a dual-boot (or bigger multi-boot) system, with a default action to be performed if no response is received within a certain amount of time.

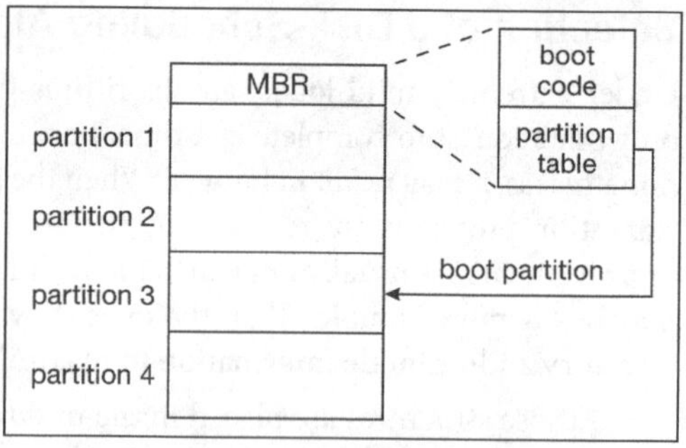

Fig.4.22.

Once the kernel has been found, the boot program loads it into memory before transferring control to the operating system. The kernel normally initializes all important kernel data structures, launches essential system services (such scheduling, init, network daemons, etc.), and then shows one or more login prompts to finish the boot process. There may now be single-user booting options, also referred to as maintenance or safe booting, in which only a small number of system functions are started. System administrators are supposed to use these modes to address problems or perform other system maintenance.

Bad Blocks

All physical items deteriorate with time, and no disk can be produced to exacting standards. Because of these factors, every disk comes with a few defective blocks, and more blocks are likely to gradually deteriorate. The entire disk will need to be replaced if many of the blocks fail, but a few here and there can be fixed in various ways.

In the past, bad blocks had to be manually checked for. The drive would be formatted or specialized disk-analysis tools would be used to identify bad blocks, after which they would repeatedly try to read the data off of them one more time. The troublesome blocks would then be located and eliminated from future use. Sometimes the data was lost forever, and other times it might have been recovered. Instruments used in disk analysis might be either destructive or nondestructive. Modern disk controllers make far better use of error-correcting codes, which enable the recovery of the majority of data and the early identification of faulty blocks. The OS's disk scheduling optimization may be affected if sectors are remapped from their typical linear progression, particularly if the replacement sector is physically distant from the sector it is replacing. Because of this, most disks typically have at least one spare cylinder and a few spare sectors on each cylinder. Abad sectors will, whenever feasible, be mapped to other sectors on the same cylinder, or at the very least, a cylinder that is as close as feasible. In order to preserve the linear evolution of sector numbers, sector slipping—which involves moving all sectors between the bad sector and the replacement sector down by one—can also be used. If a faulty block's data cannot be restored, then a hard error has occurred. Which requires replacing the file(s) from backups, or rebuilding them from scratch.

UNIT 5

Unix

5.1 UNIX COMPONENTS

Unix is a powerful and versatile operating system consisting multiple essential elements that cooperate to control the system's hardware resources and offer various services to users and applications. These components include:

1. Kernel

The kernel is the central part of Unix, responsible for managing system resources like memory, processes, hardware devices, and input/output operations.

It operates in kernel mode, which allows it to have full access to all system resources, ensuring effective resource management and protection between processes.

2. Shell

The shell provides a command-line interface that enables users to interact with the operating system by typing commands.

It serves as the user interface to the system and processes commands from the user.

Popular examples include Bash, Zsh, and Tcsh, and the shell also supports scripting for automating repetitive tasks.

3. File System

The file system organizes and manages how data is stored and accessed on disk or other storage devices.

Unix uses a tree-like hierarchical structure starting from the root directory (`/`), where files and directories are organized.

It supports various file operations like creating, deleting, and managing file permissions, along with special files like symbolic links and device files.

4. System Libraries

System libraries contain reusable code that programs use to perform common operations, such as memory allocation or file handling.

These libraries allow applications to communicate with the operating system without going through the kernel directly.

One common library is libc (C Standard Library), which provides a range of functions for system and application development.

5. Utilities/Commands

Unix comes with a broad array of command-line tools for handling tasks such as file manipulation, process management, and networking.Utilities like `ls`, `cp`, `rm`, `grep`, and `ps` help users perform a wide range of actions on files and processes, following the Unix philosophy of small, specialized programs that can be combined in scripts.

6. Device Drivers

Devicedrivers allow Unix to communicate withhardware components such as printers, hard drives, and network devices.

In Unix, device drivers are often represented as files within the `/dev` directory, enabling smooth interaction with various hardware devices.

7. Process Management

Unix supports multitasking, enabling multiple processes to run concurrently on the system.

The process scheduler allocates resources to running processes, while tools like `ps`, `top`, and `kill` allow users to manage, monitor, and terminate processes as needed.

8. Networking

Unixhas strong networkingcapabilities, supporting a variety of protocols like TCP/IP for communication across networks.

Tools like `ifconfig`, `ping`, and `netstat` help configure network interfaces and monitor network activity, facilitating communication between Unix systems and other machines.

9. Management of Users and Permissions

Because Unix is a multi-user operating system, multiple users can access and use the system at once. With the use of user management tools like `useradd`, `chmod`, and `passwd`, administrators may manage user accounts, permissions, and system resource access.

A system of read, write, and execute rights for the owner, group, and others is used by Unix file permissions.

10. Inter-Process Communication (IPC)

Unix has a number of techniques that let processes communicate with each other or synchronize, such as:

Pipes: Enable one process to pass output directly to another process as input. Message Queues: Used for sending messages between processes.

Shared memory allows many programs to access the same section of memory. Semaphores: Provide synchronization to control access to resources between processes.

11. System Calls

System calls act as the interface through which user-level programs request services from the kernel, such as creating processes, handling files, or managing memory.

These calls allow user programs to interact with the operating system at a low level, ensuring efficient communication between software and hardware.

System calls act as the interface through which user-level programs request services from the kernel, such as creating processes, handling files, or managing memory.

These calls allow user programs to interact with the operating system at a low level, ensuring efficient communication between software and hardware Together, these components make Unix a highly efficient, flexible, and secure operating system. Its design encourages modularity, which allows users and developers to interact with and manage the system easily and effectively.

5.2 INTERNAL AND EXTERNAL COMMANDS

In Unix-like operating systems, commands are categorized as internal and external based on whether they are built into the shell or stored as separate executable files on the system.

1. Internal Commands

Definition

Internal commands are a fundamental component of the shell's operation and are directly integrated into the shell. These commands are not separate programs or files but are implemented within the shell.

Execution

These commands are faster because the shell runs them directly rather than starting a new process.

Examples

- \`cd\` (Change directory): Allows users to navigate the file system.
- \`echo\` (Display a message): Prints text or output to the terminal.

The current directory path is shown by using -\`pwd\` (Print working directory).

- \`exit\` (Exit the shell): Ends the current shell session.
- \`history\` (View command history): Lists commands previously executed in the session.
- \`set\` (Set variables): Configures shell settings or variables. Characteristics:
- These commands are part of the shell itself, so they execute without the need to start a new process.
- They are available in all shell sessions and run almost instantly.

2. External Commands

Definition

External commands are separate executable programs or scripts that are stored on the system's file storage. These commands are not part of the shell but exist as standalone programs.

Execution

The shell looks for an external command in the directories listed in the PATH environment variable before executing it. The shell launches a new process to execute the command if it locates it.

Examples

- `ls` (List directory contents): Shows the files and directories within a specified directory.
- `cp` (Copy files): Used to copy files or directories from one location to another.
- `rm`(Remove files): Deletes files or directories.
- `grep` (Search for text patterns): Searches for specific strings within files or input.
- `cat` (Concatenate files): Displays the content of a file.
- `ps` (Process status): Displays a list of running processes.

Characteristics

These commands exist as files in system directories such as `/bin`,

`/usr/bin`, or others listed in the PATH.

Execution is slower than internal commands because the shell must start a new process to run them.

Key Differences Between two Commands

Aspect	Internal Commands	External Commands
Location	Built into the shell	Stored as executable files on the files system
Execution	Executed directly by the shell without creating a new process	Requires the shell to spawn a new process to rn the command
Performance	Executes quickly since no new process is created	Slower, as it requires the shell to create a new process and load the executable
Availability	Always available as long as the shell is running	Available only if the command's location is in the **PATH** directories
Examples	cd, echo, exit, pwd	ls, cp, grep, cat, ps

Summary

Internal commands are built into the shell and execute without launching additional processes, making them faster. They provide basic functionality for interacting with the system.External commands are standalone programs that must be found and executed by creating a new process. They offer a broader range of functionalities and are essential for more complex tasks.

5.3 FILE AND DIRECTORY RELATED COMMANDS

Commands Related to Files

Command	Purpose
cd	Changes the current working directory to a specified one.
pwd	Displays the full path of the current working directory.

Command	Purpose
rmdir	Eliminates an empty directory.
rm -r	Recursively deletes a directory and all of its contents.
ls -d	Lists only directories, without displaying their contents.
find	Searches for files and directories based on specific criteria, such as name or size.
tree	Visualizes the directory structure in a tree-like format.

Directory Management Commands

Command	Purpose
cd	Modifies the current working directory to a designated location.
pwd	Shows the complete path of the current working directory.
mkdir	Establishes a new directory.
rmdir	Removes an empty directory.
rm -r	Deletes a directory along with all its contents in a recursive manner.
ls -d	Displays only directories omitting their contents.
find	Locates files and directories according to specified parameters, such as name or size.
tree	Represent the directory structure in a hierarchical format.

Additional Useful Commands for Files and Directories

Command	Purpose
chmod	Alters a file or directory's permissions.
chown	Changes the owner (user or group) of a file or directory.
chgrp	Modifies a file or directory's group ownership.
stat	Displays detailed information about a file or directory, including size and timestamps.

Command	Purpose
ln	Creates a link (either hard or symbolic) to a file.
which	Shows the full path of an executable file.
basename	Extracts the base file name from a file path.
dirname	Extracts the directory path from a file path.

5.4 FILE PERMISSION AND MANIPULATION

File permission and manipulation are crucial aspects of working with files in an operating system, especially in Unix-based systems like Linux and macOS. Effective file organization and security management require an understanding of how to modify files and set permissions.

File Permissions in Unix-like Systems

In Unix-like systems, each file has a collection of permissions that limit what can be done with it. These permissions are allocated to three categories of users.

- Owner (User) : The person who owns the file.
- Group : A group of users that are assigned to the file.
- All individuals who do not possess ownership or membership within the group..

Each file permission is represented by three type :

- Read (r) : Allows reading the file.
- Write (w) : Allows modifying or deleting the file.
- Execute (x) : Allows executing the file (if it's a script or program).

Example : -rwxr-xr

This is a typical output from the ls -l command, showing the permissions of a file

The first character shows the file type. A -indicates it's a regular file. Other characters may indicate directories (d) or symbolic links (l).

rwx: Read, write, and execute permissions for the owner. r-x: Group permissions (read and execute only, no write). r--: Read-only permissions for others.

Changing Permissions

File permissions can be modified by utilizing the chmod command. There are two ways to use it: symbolic mode and numeric mode.

1. Symbolic Mode

- Syntax : chmod [who][operation][permission] filename
- Who : The users (owner, group, others) are specified. Use a (all), g (group), o (others), or u (user/owner).
- Operation : Defines what to do (add +, remove -, or set exactly =).

- Permission: The permission (read for r, write for w, and execute for x). For instance:

chmod u+x file.txt → Grants the file owner the ability to execute. chmod g-w file.txt → Removes write permission from the group. Chmod a=r file.txt → Makes everyone's permissions read-only.

2. Numeric Mode

Numbers can also be used to set permissions. Every permit has a number that goes with it Read (r) = 4.

Write (w) = 2.

Run (x) = 1.

To get the desired permissions, you add up the values. For example:

7 = 4 + 2 + 1 (read, write, and execute).

6 = 4 + 2 (read and write).

5 = 4 + 1 (read and execute).

Example :

chmod 755 file.txt → Gives read, write, and execute permissions to the owner (7), and read and execute permissions to the group and others (5).

File Manipulation

File manipulation involves commands that allow you to interact with files in various ways, such as copying, moving, renaming, and deleting.

Common Commands for File Manipulation

1. ls: Lists files and directories in a directory.

For instance, ls -l → Lists comprehensive data, such as file size, permissions, and modification date.

2. Cp : Copies files or directories.

Example : cp file1.txt file2.txt → Copies file1.txt to file2.txt.

3. Mv : Moves or renames files.

Example : mv file1.txt /path/to/directory/ → Moves file1.txt to another directory. Example : mv oldname.txt newname.txt → Renames a file.

4. Rm : Removes files or directories.

Example : rm file.txt → Deletes file.txt. Warning : rm permanently deletes the file, so be cautious.

5. Touch: Create a brand-new, blank file.

The touch command can be used to create a brand-new, blank file or to update the timestamp of an existing file.

Example :

touch newfile.txt → Creates an empty file named newfile.txt.

6. Cat : Displays the contents of a file.

Example :

cat file.txt → Prints the contents of file.txt to the terminal.

7. Chmod : Changes the permissions of a file (as described earlier).

8. To change who owns a file or directory, use the 'chown' command.

For instance, chown user1 file.txt → Modifies the file.txt's owner to user1.

For instance, chown user1:group1 file.txt → Modifies the group to group1 and the owner to user1.

9. Chgrp: Adjusts the group ownership linked to a directory or file.

For instance, chgrp group1 file.txt → Modifies file.txt's group ownership to group1.

Directory Manipulation

Just like files, directories can also be manipulated.

- mkdir:Establishes a fresh directory.
  - As an illustration, mkdir new_folder → generates a directory with the name new_folder.
- rmdir: Gets rid of a blank directory.
  - As an illustration, rmdir old_folder → deletes the old_folder directory, provided it is empty.
- rm -r: Gets rid of a directory and everything in it.
  - Example : rm -r folder_name → Deletes folder_name and everything inside

Example Use Cases :

Changing File Permissions :

```
chmod 644 file.txt
```

Copying Files : To copy file1.txt to a backup directory

```
cp file1.txt /path/to/backup/
```

Rename Files : To rename a file :

```
mv old_file.txt new_file.txt
```

Removing Files : To delete a file :

```
rm file.txt
```

Changing Ownership : To change the owner of a file to user1 and the group to staff :

```
chown user1:staff file.txt
```

By combining file permissions and manipulation commands, Access to files and folders can be managed, ensure security, and organize files effectively. Let me know if you'd like to explore any specific commands or scenarios in more detail!

5.5 STANDARD I/O

Standard I/O (Input/Output) in Unix-like Systems

In Unix-like operating systems, Standard Input (stdin), Standard Output (stdout), and Standard Error (stderr) are the three default communication channels used by programs and the shell to interact with the user and other programs. These are fundamental concepts for working with the command line and for handling file operations and data flow.

Here's a breakdown of Standard I/O :

Standard Input (stdin) :

- Standard Input (stdin) is the default source of input data for a program.
- It is typically the keyboard, but can also be redirected from a file or another program.
- File descriptor: 0
- Command-line behavior : When you run a program in the shell, it usually waits for input from

```
$ cat
Hello, world!
```

stdin (e.g., typing data into the terminal).

In this example, cat waits for input from the terminal (stdin). Whatever you type will be echoed back to the terminal.

You can also redirect input from a file :

By doing this, the contents of file.txt will be redirected to the cat command's stdin.

```
$ cat < file.txt
```

Standard Output (stdout) :

- The default location for program output data is Standard Output (stdout)..
- It is typically the terminal screen but can also be redirected to a file or another program.
- File descriptor : 1

The echo command sends its output to stdout, which by default is the terminal. You can redirect the output to a file :

```
$ echo "Hello, world!"
Hello, world!
```

In this instance, the message "Hello, world!" The information is directed to the output. txt file rather than being displayed in the terminal.

```
$ echo "Hello, world!" > output.txt
```

Error Standard (stderr) :

The default location for error messages or diagnostic output from a program is Standard Error (stderr). Just like stdout, stderr is typically the terminal, but it can also be redirected to a file or another program. File descriptor : 2

```
$ ls non_existent_file
ls: cannot access 'non_existent_file': No such file or directory
```

Here, the error message is printed to stderr. You can redirect stderr to a file :

```
$ ls non_existent_file 2> error.log
```

In this case, Rather of being shown on the screen, the error message is recorded to error.log. Redirection :

Redirection allows you to change where input and output data come from and go to.

- Input Redirection : Takes input from a file and sends it to stdin. Example :

```
command < input.txt
```

This sends the contents of input.txt to stdin of command.

Output Redirection : Sends output from output to a file rather than the screen.

Example :

```
command > output.txt
```

This sends the output of command to output.txt.

- Error Redirection : Sends error messages from stderr to a file. Example :

```
command 2> error.txt
```

Redirecting Both stdout and stderr : Both output and errors can be redirected to the same file.

```
command > output.txt 2>&1
```

Example :

Aspect	Internal Commands	External Commands
Location	Built into the shell	Stored as executable files on the files system
Execution	Executed directly by the shell without creating a new process	Requires the shell to spawn a new process to rn the command
Performance	Executes quickly since no new process is created	Slower, as it requires the shell to create a new process and load the executable
Availability	Always available as long as the shell is running	Available only if the command's location is in the **PATH** directories
Examples	cd, echo, exit, pwd	ls, cp, grep, cat, ps

This causes output.txt to be the new location for both stdout and stderr.

- Appending Output to a File : Use >> to append data to an existing file. Example :

```
command >> output.txt
```

Pipes

A pipe (|) is used to send the output (stdout) of one command to the input (stdin) of another command.This enables the combination of several commands in succession.

```
$ ls | grep "file"
```

Here the grep command receives the output of the ls command (list of files) as input, which then filters and shows only the lines containing the word "file".

File Descriptors

In Unix-like systems, file descriptors are integer handles that represent open files. These are: Standard Input (stdin) is represented by 0;

Standard Output (stdout) by 1; and Standard Error (stderr) by 2.

You can use file descriptors in redirection and piping operations. For example :

- Redirecting stdin from a file :

```
command < input.txt
```

- Redirecting stdout to a file :

```
command > output.txt
```

- Redirecting stderr to a file :

```
command 2> error.txt
```

- Redirecting both stdout and stderr :

```
command > output.txt 2>&1
```

Common Commands Using Standard I/O

Echo : Sends data to stdout.

```
echo "Hello, World!"
```

Cat : Reads from stdin and sends to stdout.

```
cat < input.txt
```

Grep : Reads from stdin and filters data.

```
cat file.txt | grep "pattern"
```

Tee: Writes to a file and stdout after reading from stdin.

```
echo "Hello, World!" | tee output.txt
```

Sort: Writes to stdout after reading from stdin and sorting the data.

```
cat file.txt | sort
```

Examples of Redirection and Pipelines

Example 1 : Redirecting stdout to a file

Rather than printing "This is a test" to the terminal, this will send it to output.txt.

```
$ echo "This is a test" > output.txt
```

Example 2: Pointing to a file with stderr

Error.log will receive the error message.

```
$ ls non_existent_file 2> error.log
```

Example 3 : Piping commands

The contents of file.txt are passed through grep to find lines with "example" and then sorted.

```
$ cat file.txt | grep "example" | sort
```

Summary

- Standard Input (stdin) : Default input source (usually the keyboard).
- Standard Output (stdout) : Default output destination (usually the terminal).
- Standard Error (stderr) : Default destination for error messages.
- Redirection : Allows input or output to be directed to/from files.
- Pipes : Enable the chaining of commands by utilizing one command's output as another's input.

Understanding how to manipulate Standard I/O is essential for efficient shell scripting and system administration. Should you require additional information or examples, please do not hesitate to inquire.

5.6 CONFIGURING VI ENVIRONMENT

In addition to using configurations from your shell, the vi editor can also read settings from a text file. We will guide you through some common configuration options you might find helpful. To configure vi :

1. Open your ~/.exrc file using vi.
2. Add the desired settings. For instance, to show the current mode (either insert or command) in the status line, which is very helpful for novices, use :
3. set showmode
4. If you want to enable word wrapping (indicated by wm), and prefer it to activate within five characters from the screen's right border, such as the line that follows:
5. set wm=5
6. To set the tab stop to every four spaces instead of the default eight, add :
7. set tabstop=4

The table outlines several common vi configuration options. Be sure to consult the vi manual page for a complete list.

Common vi Configuration Settings

Configuration Option	Setting	Description
Show current mode	set showmode	Displays the current mode (command or insert) in the status line.
Word wrapping	set wm=5	Enables word wrapping, starting 5 characters from the right edge.
Tab stop	set tabstop=4	Sets the tab stop to 4 spaces instead of the default 8.

Line numbering	set number	Shows line numbers on the left side for easier navigation.
Auto indentation	set smartindent set autoindent	Enables automatic indentation for easier coding.
Syntax highlighting	syntax on	Enables syntax highlighting for easier reading and editing.
Search highlighting	set insearch set hlsearch	Highlights search matches and shows results as you type.
File format	set fileformat=unix	Specifies the default file format (e.g. unix or dos).

Commands for Saving/Exiting:

- Save and exit: :wq
- Exit without saving: :q!

The new configurations will take effect the next time you launch vi.

5.7 REGULAR EXPRESSIONS IN UNIX

Regular expressions (regex) are powerful tools in Unix-based systems, enabling efficient searching, matching, and manipulation of text patterns. These expressions are supported by numerous utilities, including grep, sed, awk, and other text-processing tools. Below is an overview of how regular expressions function in Unix and how to use them effectively.

What is a Regular Expression?

It is employed to look for or match particular patterns in input streams, files, or strings.In Unix, regular expressions are widely employed for tasks such as searching, filtering, and editing text.

Types of Regular Expressions in Unix

Unix systems support two types of regular expressions :

- **Basic Regular Expressions (BRE) :** This is the default mode for tools like grep, sed, and awk.
- **Extended Regular Expressions (ERE) :** An advanced version with more features, commonly used in utilities like egrep or when sed is run with the -E option.

BRE vs ERE

- In Basic Regular Expressions (BRE), some special characters. It is required that a backslash (\) come before ?, +, {}, |, and ().
- In Extended Regular Expressions (ERE), these characters can be used without escaping them.

Basic Syntax of Regular Expressions

Here are some common elements you will encounter in regular expressions :

Literal Characters

Literal characters match themselves directly, such as letters or symbols like a, b, 1, @. Example: a matches the letter `a'.

Metacharacters

Metacharacters are symbols with special meanings in regex. Here's a breakdown:

Metacharacters: Metacharacters are symbols with special meanings in regex. Here's a breakdown:

- **Dot (.):** Matches any single character except a newline.
  Example: a.c , matches abc , axc , a1c , etc.
- **Caret (^):** matches the beginning of a line.
  Example: ^abc matches lines starting with abc .
- **Dollar Sign ($):** Matches the end of a line.
  Example: abc$ matches lines ending with abc .
- **Asterisk (*):** Matches zero or more occurrences of the preceding character or group.
  Example: a* , matches", a , aa , aaa , etc.
- **Plus (+):** Matches one or more repetitions of the preceding character or group (in ERE).
  Example: a+ matches a , aa , aaa , etc. (but not an empty string).
- **Question Mark (?):** Matches zero or one repetition of the preceding character or group (in ERE).
  Example: a? matches a or " (empty string).
- **Brackets ([]):** Define a character class, matching any one of the characters within the brackets.
  Example: [abc] matches a , b , or c .
- **Carets inside Brackets ([^]):** Negates the character class, meaning it matches anything except the characters inside.
  Example: [^abc] matches any character except a , b , or c .
- **Parentheses (()):** Used for grouping expressions together (in ERE), allowing you to apply quantifiers to the entire group.
  Example: (ab)+ matches ab , abab , ababab , etc.
- **Pipe (|):** Represents alternatin (OR) between different expressions (in ERE).

Character Classes

A group of characters enclosed in square brackets [] is called a character class. It allows you to match any character from a specific group.

Predefined classes

- \d: Matches any digit (0-9).
- \ w: corresponds to words (letters, numbers, accents) in the symbol.
- \ s: corresponds to all space symbols (spaces, tabs, new lines). Character ranges :
- [a-z]: Matches any lowercase letter.
- [A-Z]: Matches any uppercase letter.
- [0-9]: Matches any digit.
- [a-zA-Z0-9]: Matches any alphanumeric character.

Quantifiers

The number of instances of a character or group that must match is specified via quantifiers :

* : 0 or more.

+ : 1 or more.

? : 0 or 1.

{n} : Exactly n occurrences. Example : a{3} matches exactly aaa.

{n,} : n or more occurrences.

Example : a{3,} matches aaa, aaaa, aaaaa, etc.

{n,m} : Between n and m occurrences. Example : a{2,4} matches aa, aaa, or aaaa.

Using Regular Expressions in Unix Tools

grep (Search for Patterns in Files)

grep is the most commonly used tool for searching text patterns in files. It supports both Regular expressions can be classified as either Basic (BRE) or Extended (ERE).

```
grep 'pattern' filename
```

- Using Extended Regular Expressions (ERE) with grep:

```
grep-E 'pattern' filename
```

- Invert match:

```
grep-v 'pattern' filename
```

- Case-insensitive search:

```
grep-i 'pattern' filename
```

Stream Editor (sed)

Sed is a stream editor that uses regular expressions to change text.

- Basic substitution
- Global substitution: Replace all occurrences of a pattern in a line:
- Using Extended Regular Expressions (with -E): sed -E 's/(ab|cd)/xyz/' filename
- Awk (Pattern Scanning and Processing Language) :

Awk is a robust language for text processing that matches patterns using regular expressions. awk '/pattern/ { print $0 }' filename

Advanced Regular Expression Concepts

Look ahead and Look behind (Not supported in all tools) :

Look aheads and look behinds allow you to assert a pattern exists (or doesn't exist) before or after another pattern. These are supported in Perl Compatible Regular Expressions (PCRE), but not in basic Unix tools like grep or sed.

Greedy vs. Non-Greedy Matching

By default, * and + are greedy. You can make them non-greedy (or lazy) by appending a ? after the quantifier. Example: a.b (greedy) vs. a.*?b (non-greedy).

5.8 PROCESS-RELATED COMMANDS

In Unix-based systems, processes are crucial for managing tasks. Processes represent running programs and can be controlled using various commands. Here's an overview of some essential process-related commands in Unix.

1. *ps* -Display Status of the Process

On UNIX systems, processes can be viewed with the "PS" command. By default, it provides instantaneous processes associated with the current port session.

- Basic Syntax : `ps`
- Common Options :
  - `ps -e` or `ps -A` : Displays all processes running on the system.
  - `ps -u username` : Shows processes owned by a specific user.
  - `ps aux` : Displays detailed information about all running processes.
  - `ps -f` : Shows a full listing with extra details about processes.

top -Display Active Processes

It displays the most CPU-intensive tasks and updates the information periodically.

- Basic Syntax : Top
- Usage Tips : To quit, press q.

You can press specific keys within top to sort processes by CPU or memory usage.

- Kill: Stop Procedures

Signals to the processes are sent using the "Kill" command, usually to stop them. The processes can be interrupted by indicating their process identifier (PID).

- Basic Syntax : Killall-Name-Based Process Termination. By giving the program's name instead of its PID, the killall command enables you to end processes.
- Common Options :
  - `kill -9 PID` : Gracefully terminate the process (SIGKILL).
  - `kill -15 PID` : Gracefully terminate the process (SIGTERM).

- Basic Syntax :

```
killall process_name
```

- bg -Resume Process in Background :
- The bg command resumes a suspended process and runs it in the background.
- Basic Syntax :

```
bg %job_number
```

fg -Bring Process to The foreground

A background process is brought to the foreground via the fg command, allowing it to interact directly with the user.

- Basic Syntax :

```
fg %job_number
```

- Usage Example : If a process is running in the background, using fg will bring it back to the foreground.
- Basic Syntax :

```
nice -n priority command
```

- Example :

```
nice -n10myprogram
```

- nice-Set Process Priority : To start a process with a specific priority. The priority is measured on a scale with the highest priority at –20 and the lowest priority at 19.

2. renice -Change Priority of Running Process

The renice command is used to change the priority of an already running process by specifying its PID.

- Basic Syntax:

```
renice priority PID
```

- Example:

```
renice -5 1234
```

3. nohup -Run a Process Immune to Hangups

The nohup command is used to run a command without the process being terminated when the user logs out or the terminal is closed.

- Basic Syntax:

```
nohup command &
```

- Example:

```
nohup long_running_command &
```

4. jobs -List Background Jobs

The jobs command displays a list of all jobs running in the current shell session, including both foreground and background jobs.

- Basic Syntax :

```
jobs
```

5. wait -Wait for Process Completion

The wait command waits for a process to finish before continuing with the execution of subsequent commands. It is often used in scripts.

- Basic Syntax :

```
wait PID
```

6. pstree -Display Procedures as a Tree

Processes are displayed in a tree-like form using the pstree command, displaying the relationship between parent and child processes.

- Basic Syntax :

```
pstree
```

Proper use of these commands allows users to efficiently monitor, control, and optimize system tasks.

5.9 SHELL PROGRAMMING

Introduction

An interface between the user and the UNIX operating system is called a shell. Shell programming involves writing scripts using shell commands to automate tasks.

Types of UNIX Shells

- Bash (Bourne Again Shell) – An improved version of Bourne shell with added features.
- C Shell (csh) – Uses C-like syntax, preferred by programmers.
- Korn Shell (ksh) – Combines features of Bourne and C Shell.

Advantages of Shell Scripting

- Automates repetitive tasks.
- Simplifies complex system administration.
- Reduces manual errors.
- Enhances system performance through efficient scripting.

Shell Script Basics

- A file with a series of shell commands is called a shell script.
- Scripts are executed by the shell interpreter.
- The first line of a shell script specifies the interpreter: #!/bin/bash

Variables in Shell Scripting

- User-defined Variables:

```
name="John"
echo "Hello, $name"
```

Shell Script Execution

- Run the script using:

```
./script.sh
```

- Or execute with a specific shell:

```
bash script.sh
```

5.10 BRANCHING CONTROL STRUCTURES

In Unix operating systems, branching control structures are essential for executing commands conditionally in shell scripts. They allow the system to guide the execution process by making judgments based on predetermined criteria. In Unix shell scripting, the primary branching control structures that are utilized are :

5.10.1 If-Else Statements

The if statement is used to execute a block of code only if a condition evaluates as true. You can also use else to run a different block of code if the condition is false.

if [condition]; then

commands executed if the condition true elif [another_condition]; then # commands executed if the second condition is true else

commands executed if none of the conditions are true fi Example :

#!/bin/bash

if [-f "file.txt"]; then echo "file.txt exists." else

echo "file.txt doesn't exist." fi

In this script, if the file file.txt is present, the script will output file.txt exists; if not, the file will be printed. There isn't a text message.

5.10.2 Case Statement

The case statement is ideal when you need to check a variable against multiple possible patterns. It's a more efficient way of handling many conditions compared to multiple if statements.

```
case "$variable" in pattern1)
        # commands to execute if pattern1 matches
        ;;
    pattern2)
        # commands to execute if pattern2 matches
        ;;
    *)
        # commands to execute if no pattern matches
        ;;
```

```
esac
# ASR the user to input a number between 1 and 7
echo "Please enter a number between 1 and 7 to know the corresponding
day of the week:"
read day_number
# Use the case statement to check the input and display the day
case $day_number in
    1)
        echo "Monday"
        ;;
    2)
        echo "Tuesday"
        ;;
    3)
        echo "Wednesday"
        ;;
    4)
        echo "Thursday"
        ;;
    5)
        echo "Friday"
        ;;
    6)
        echo "Saturday"
        ;;
    7)
        echo "Sunday"
        ;;
    *)
        echo "That's not a valid input. Please enter a number between
        1 and 7."
        ;;
esac
```

5.10.3 Short-Circuit Conditional Expression

While Unix shell scripting does not have a direct ternary operator like some other languages, you can mimic ternary behavior using the && (AND) and || (OR) operators to evaluate a condition and run commands based on the result.

Syntax :

```
[condition] && command_if_true || command_if_false
```

Example :

In this example, if file.txt exists, the script will display "file.txt exists." If it doesn't, it will display "file.txt does not exist."

5.11 LOOP CONTROL STRUCTURES

While And Until Loops

Although not strictly branching, loops often use conditional expressions to repeatedly execute code based on certain criteria.

While Loop

- The while loop execute as long as the condition is true.

```
#!/bin/bash
counter=1
while [ $counter -le 5 ]; do
    echo "Counter is $counter"
    ((counter++))
done
```

- An until loop executes as long as the condition remains false.

```
#!/bin/bash
counter=1
until [ $counter -gt 5 ]; do
    echo "Counter is $counter"
    ((counter++))
done
```

For Loop

In Unix shell scripting, loop control structures allow you to repeat a set of instructions multiple times, which is especially useful for automating tasks. The for loop is one of the most commonly used loops in shell scripts. It enables you to iterate over a sequence of values and perform operations on each item in that sequence.

Basic for Loop with a Range of Numbers

A common usage of the for loop is to repeat a set of commands for a sequence of numbers.

Syntax :

```
for variable in {start..end}
do
    # commands to execute for each iteration
done
```

Example :

```
#!/bin/bash
# Loop from 1 to 5
for i in {1..5}
do
    echo "iteration number: $i"
done
```

For Loop With A List Of Items

You can also use a for loop to iterate over a predefined list of items, such as names, strings, or file names.

Syntax :

```
for item in item1 item2 item3 ...
do
    # commands to execute for each item
done
```

Example :

```
#!/bin/bash
# Loop over a list of weekdays
for day in Monday Tuesday Wednesday Thursday Friday
do
    echo "Today is $day"
done
```

C-Style For Loop

The for loop in this form is similar to loops in languages like C, where you specify an initialization, condition, and increment directly in the loop structure.

Syntax :

```
for ((initialization; condition; increment))
do
    # commands to execute for each iteration
done
```

Example :

```
#!/bin/bash
# Loop from 1 to 5 using C-style syntax
for ((i=1; i<=5; i++))
do
    echo "Number: $i"
done
```

Here, the loop starts with i=1, and increments i after each iteration, continuing until i exceeds 5.

Looping Over Files In A Directory

A useful application of the for loop is iterating over files in a directory, which allows you to perform actions on each file.

Syntax :

```
for file in /path/to/directory/*
do
    # commands to process each file
done
```

Example :

```
#!/bin/bash
# Loop through all files in the current directory
for file in *
do
    echo "Processing file: $file"
    # Additional commands to process the file
done
```

5.12 JUMPING CONTROL STRUCTURES

Jumping control structures allow programs to change the normal sequence of execution. These structures enable skipping, looping, or exiting code blocks based on conditions or predefined logic.

5.12.1 Break Statement

The break statement is used to immediately terminate the execution of a loop or a switch-case structure. When encountered, the program exits the loop or switch block and continues with the next statement outside of it.

Usage In Loops

In looping structures like for, while, and do-while, the break statement helps in stopping the loop execution before it naturally ends

Example : Using break in a for Loop

```
#include <stdio.h>

int main() {
  for (int i = 0; i < 5; i++) {
    if (i == 3) {
      break; // Stops the loop when i equals 3
    }
    printf("%d ", i);
  }
  return 0;
}
```

Output : 0 1 2

Here, the loop terminates as soon as i reaches 3, skipping further iterations.

Example : Using break in a while Loop :

```
#include <stdio.h>

int main() {
  int i = 0;
  while (i < 5) {
    if (i == 3) {
      break; // Exits Loop when i is 3
    }
    printf("%d ", i);
    i++;
  }
  return 0;
}
```

Output : 0 1 2

Usage in Switch Statements

In a switch statement, break is used to exit the block once a case is executed, preventing the execution of subsequent cases.

Example : Using break in a switch Statement

```
#include <stdio.h>

int main() {
  int num = 2;
  switch (num) {
    case 1:
      printf("One\n");
      break;
    case 2:
      printf("Two\n");
      break;
    case 3:
      printf("Three\n");
      break;
    default:
      printf("Other number\n");
  }
  return 0;
}
```

Output : Two

Without the break statement, execution would continue into the next cases, leading to unintended results.

5.12.2 Continue Statement

The continue statement skip the current iteration of a loop and move to the next iteration. Unlike the break statement, which exits the loop entirely, continue allows the loop to keep running while skipping specific conditions.

Example : continue in a for Loop: Output : 0 1 3 4

```
#include <stdio.h>

int main() {
  for (int i = 0; i < 5; i++) {
    if (i == 2) {
      continue; // Skips the iteration when i is 2
    }
    printf("%d ", i);
  }
  return 0;
}
```

In this example, when i equals 2, the continue statement is executed, skipping the printf statement for that iteration. The loop then proceeds with the next value.

Example : continue in a while Loop

```
#include <stdio.h>

int main() {
  int i = 0;
  while (i < 5) {
    i++;
    if (i == 3) {
      continue; // Skips printing when i is 3
    }
    printf("%d ", i);
  }
  return 0;
}
```

Output : 1 2 4 5

Here, when i equals 3, For that iteration, printf is skipped and the continue statement is run.

The exit Statement

The exit statement is used to terminate a program immediately. When executed, it stops all further code execution and returns control to the operating system

Syntax :

```
#include <stdlib.h>
exit(status_code);
```

- The status_code is an integer value returned to the operating system.
  - exit(0) : Indicates successful program termination.
  - exit(1) or any non-zero value : Indicates abnormal termination (error occurred).

Usage of exit in a Program

Example : Exiting on an Error Condition

```
#include <stdio.h>
#include <stdlib.h>

int main() {
  int number;
  printf("Enter a positive number: ");
  scanf("%d", &number);

  if (number < 0) {
    printf("Error: Negative number entered.\n");
    exit(1); // Terminates the program with an error status
  }

  printf("You entered: %d\n", number);
  return 0;
}
```

Output (if user enters -5) :

Error : Negative number entered.

The program stops execution immediately after calling exit(1).

Example : Using exit(0) for Normal Termination :

```
#include <stdio.h>
#include <stdlib.h>

int main() {
  printf("Program started.\n");

  exit(0); // Ends the program normally

  printf("This will never be printed.\n"); // Unreachable code
  return 0;
}
```

Output :

Program started.

Since exit(0) is called, the last printf statement is never executed. Integer and Floating-Point Arithmetic in Shell

5.13 INTEGER AND REAL ARITHMETIC IN SHELL PROGRAMS SCRIPTING

Shell scripts support arithmetic operations for both integers and floating-point numbers, but handling them requires different techniques.

1. Integer Arithmetic

Shell scripting provides multiple ways to perform arithmetic on integers, including :

expr command

$((...)) for arithmetic expansion let command bc (Basic Calculator)

Example 1 : Performing Arithmetic with expr

```
#!/bin/bash
num1=10
num2=5

sum=$(expr $num1 + $num2)
echo "Sum: $sum"
```

Output :

Sum : 15

Example 2 : Using $((...)) for Arithmetic Expansion

```
sh
#!/bin/bash
num1=10
num2=5

sum=$((num1 + num2))
difference=$((num1 -num2))
product=$((num1 * num2))
quotient=$((num1 / num2)) # Integer division

echo "Sum: $sum; Difference: $difference; Product: $product; Quotient:
$quotient"
```

Output :

Sum: 15, Difference: 5, Product: 50, Quotient: 2

Note : Since the shell does not support floating-point numbers in arithmetic expansion, division results in integer values.

Example 3 : Arithmetic Using let

```
#!/bin/bash
num1=8
num2=3
let sum=num1+num2
let difference=num1-num2
echo "Sum: $sum, Difference: $difference"
```

2. Floating-Point Arithmetic

Since shell scripting does not directly handle floating-point operations, tools like bc or awk must be used.

Example 1 : Using bc for Floating-Point Calculations

```
#!/bin/bash
num1=8
num2=3

let sum=num1+num2
let difference=num1-num2

echo "Sum: $sum, Difference: $difference"
```

Output :

Sum: 13.0, Product: 26.25, Quotient: 4.20

Example 2 : Using awk for Floating-Point Operations

```
#!/bin/bash
num1=5.5
num2=2.2

sum=$(awk "BEGIN {print $num1 + $num2}")
quotient=$(awk "BEGIN {print $num1 / $num2}")

echo "Sum: $sum, Quotient: $quotient"
```

Comparison of Methods

Method	Integer Arithmetic	Floating-Point Arithmetic
expr	✓ Supported	✗ Not Supported
$(( ))	✓ Supported	✗ Not Supported
let	✓ Supported	✗ Not Supported
bc	✓ Supported	✓ Supported
awk	✓ Supported	✓ Supported

◆◆◆